WHITSUNDAY'S CHILD

A COUNTRY LIFE IN PICTURES BY VERA PUNTER

Vera Punter

March 1994

This book is dedicated to the memory of my late husband, Charlie, who shared my love of Rodbourne and its peaceful countryside. We had a happy, if sometimes hard, fifty six years together and were lucky to be the centre of a loving family

WHITSUNDAY'S CHILD

A COUNTRY LIFE IN PICTURES BY VERA PUNTER

DEVISED BY SARA JANE HAGGERTY

EDITED BY JULIE WOODGATE

WITH FOREWORD BY DAVID PUTTNAM

East Herts Publishing Co Ltd

First published by East Herts Publishing Company Limited 1993.
© Vera Punter and Sara Jane Haggerty.
The authors have asserted the moral right to be identified as the authors of this work.

Published in the United Kingdom by East Herts Publishing Company Limited
57-63 Brownfields, Welwyn Garden City, Hertfordshire, AL7 1AN.
ISBN 0-9519989-1-9.
Printed and bound in Great Britain by P Linard and Co WEB Limited Wakefield
Yorkshire.
Designed and typeset by O'Brien Haggerty Design.

CONTENTS

PHOTOGRAPHS: SIAN IRVINE

Message from Penny Kitchen, editor of Home & Country, magazine for the WI

In a small way, I feel that Home & Country has helped to shorten the long gestation period normally required for a 'good idea' to become a book. We can boast of having published Vera's work first!

The real moving spirit behind the book project is Vera Punter's granddaughter, Sara Jane Haggerty, who has had an unfailing faith in the merits of Vera's life and work.

Vera, besides being a superb photographer for over fifty years, has also been an active WI member for the same period and is now a member of the Brokenborough WI, Wiltshire.

The only sadness is that Vera's late husband Charlie, the subject of so many of her pictures, didn't live to see the publication of this book. He would have been immensely proud.

ACKNOWLEDGEMENTS

VERA: Thanks to Anna and Jim and their children Sara Jane and Martin, George and Cathy and sons Colin and Marcos in Australia. Also thanks to John and Jean Herbert and Ben Barton for their help. Special thanks to granddaughter Sara Jane - without her help this book would not have materialised.

Thanks to all the folk who lived in the village in those days and were always so helpful and friendly. Very few are left now, but their descendants are scattered over England and Wales and countries abroad. Thanks to Willis Bros for their help and information, also thanks to Julie Woodgate, my co-writer, for her help and guidance.

SARA: A big thank-you to Dave Crowe, for always believing in me and the project; and to Paul Linard for publishing the work. Thank you to all who helped and encouraged me, including Colette Blanchard, Paula O'Brien, Edwin Donald, John Shirley, Dennis Hackett, Maggie Pringle, Julie Woodgate, Barbie Boxall, and my family; especially my Mum. Also, thank-you to David Puttnam who inspired me and constantly supported the book. Last, but not least, thanks to Gran for being such a brilliant Gran.

JULIE: Thanks to my late grandparents, and my father, for bringing me up on a diet of family stories and photographs, which made working on this project with Vera and Sara such a privilege and a pleasure. And to my husband, David, for putting up with me!

TOWER GROUND

MANOR FARM

HOLY ROOD CHURCH

PARSLOE FARM

TO ANGROVE →

PLOUGH INN

CROSS

VILLAGE PUMP

RODBOURNE

FIELD LANE
TO BINCOME WOOD

TRINITY FARM

SCHOOL

THE ORCHARDS

HOME Grnd.

CHURCH FARM BUILDINGS

POLES

OSBOURNES Close

POUND FARM

POUND HILL

POUND HILL COTTAGE

SOURCE OF VILLAGE DRINKING WATER

GIBBS

WORCESTERS

RODBOURNE BOTTOM FARM

SEXTONS

GODWINS FARM

ROOD BROOK

GIBBS LANE

GODDINS

RODBOURNE BOTTOM

STARTLEY Grnds.

WITHYSLABS

HILLY Grnd.

ILLUSTRATION: COLETTE BLANCHARD

8

FOREWORD

Like all worthwhile autobiography, this wonderful photographic record tells us more about the world its author inhabited than any formal history could ever hope to achieve. I know the village of Rodbourne well and have a deep affection for it. It is only a few miles from my home in one of the most beautiful corners of the largely rural county of Wiltshire. Vera Punter's 'snaps' illustrate a rich and varied story of forty years of life in Rodbourne - its joys exuberantly celebrated and its hardships faithfully recorded.

Her quality of authenticity is reminiscent of the work of John Clare, one of England's finest rural poets. He knew at first hand the unremitting hardship of living and working on the land and yet could write:

> *'O Rural Life! What charms thy meanness hide;*
> *What sweet description bards disdain to sing;'*

Vera Punter sings a song that is unsentimental but full of 'sweet description' of the joys and satisfactions of everyday life in a small and settled farming community. Many of the images are tantalisingly familiar. It's easy to forget that this is a world which, after hundreds of years of gradual evolution, was about to be turned upside down and aspects of it lost forever. First came the M4, closely followed by commuters, weekend cottages and the Common Agricultural Policy. All over England small mixed farms gave way to bigger holdings, growing specialised crops to meet largely arbitrary quotas. In thirty years, tens of thousands of miles of hedgerow were ripped out of the English countryside, countless ponds drained and coppices felled, their flora and fauna made homeless simply so that giant machines could plough and spray and harvest in straighter and, therefore, more cost-effective rows. Of course, other changes have been more welcome. John Clare drew a bitter picture of the farm worker who:

> *'Toiling in the naked fields,*
> *Where no bush or shelter yields...*
> *Beats and blows his numbing hands'*

That particular level of hardship - as familiar fifty, as it was two hundred, years ago - has also, mercifully, been consigned to the past.

Perhaps more than anything else, these photographs are a timely reminder of that powerful sense of a community in which values and responsibilities were instinctively shared. Farming was not just about producing as much food as cheaply as possible. It was also about caring for the countryside and, in doing so, caring for the Earth and for the society in which we all have a share. Those values make us feel nostalgic but that would be far too simplistic a response because there is absolutely nothing quaint about them. Indeed, if we fail to rediscover them for our own times - no matter how painful or arduous that process may be - we will continue to pay a terrible social and environmental price for that failure. In the end, like all the best history, this book tells us as much about ourselves as it does about life in rural England more than half a century ago.

PHOTOGRAPH: TVS

INTRODUCTION

When my Gran and Gramp had to move from their four-bedroomed farmhouse in the tiny Wiltshire village of Rodbourne to a one-bedroomed 'old peoples' bungalow in the nearby town of Malmesbury in 1976, there was obviously no room to house all their possessions. Some were thrown away, others were burnt, given to the family or sold. Among the things Gran decided to give me were four old albums of her own photographs that I had enjoyed looking at when I was a little girl.

I was sixteen at the time, still living at home with mum and dad in our modern 1970s council house. Although I thought the photographs were interesting, and something I should look after and keep safely because 'Gran had given them to me', I didn't really look at them very closely or show them to anybody.

The following year when I left home for art college in London, some of the few possessions that came with me in a small blue suitcase to my student accomodation were Gran's four photo albums. I can't really remember why I took them with me - although maybe it was because they reminded me of my home and childhood, and the safe, cosy feelings of being in Rodbourne.

When I eventually made some friends in the Halls of Residence where I was living, I showed them the photo albums. I remember two girls in particular, one who is still a good friend, pawing over them telling me how lucky I was to have these pictures and how most people didn't have pictures of their family like mine. I explained that Gran had taken most of the pictures and, didn't all Grans take lots of pictures like these?

They laughed, and said that they did have some old family pictures, but they just tended to focus on the odd family occasion, like a wedding, Christening or maybe a holiday and, anyway, often half the heads were chopped off, or everyone looked miserable.

I didn't think too much about this at the time, and over the next three years I left college, started work and lived in a variety of dodgy flats in south London.

I soon discovered that whoever I showed the pictures to seemed to say the same things that my college friends had said about them. They were fascinated by the clothes and hats of the 1930s and the cosy feeling and detail of the farming pictures, which showed the threshing, harvesting and day-to-day events of my Gran and Gramp's life in Rodbourne, comparing them to memories and old pictures they had of their families.

If I ever showed anybody older, nearer my Gran's age, they obviously had a different initial reaction to the pictures and they would start talking about their own families or memories. The men talked of using the same sort of farming methods as they saw being used in some of the Pound Farm pictures, or their own wartime memories. The women remembered wearing cloche hats or berets, like the ones Gran and her friends wore in the 1920s, and remembered going to dances or meeting their first boyfriends. They seemed to be reminded of happy times when they looked at the pictures, not the hard times.

Eventually, in 1987, not being able to deny my 'country' roots any longer, I moved out of London to live in a village in Kent and, of course the albums came with me and got put in a drawer with all of my own photo albums. I still regularly visited home and, more often than not, would come back up the motorway with a car boot load of stuff given to me by my mum or Gran as they are both terrible hoarders, (not like myself of course...). On one occasion in 1989, just before Christmas, while visiting the family I unexpectedly found myself loading thousands of 35mm transparencies into the boot of my car. They were contained in a big cardboard box, some sealed in plastic boxes - each one containing about thirty or forty - and some were just loose in a smaller suitcase.

Gran decided to give them to me as she said she was clearing out the 'scubhold' (junk room) one day and couldn't seem to find a home for them. She also thought I might enjoy looking at them.

11

I got them home that day and over the Christmas break, when I'd finished wrapping presents and doing festive things, I took out the small illuminated viewer she had also given me and started to have a look at some of them.

The viewer only took one transparency at a time so I decided not to look at them all at once - it looked such a daunting job! So, randomly choosing a couple of the plastic sealed containers that were full, I started to sort through, hoping to find some funny shots of me and my brother Martin when we were kids in the 1960s. I wanted to give him and his girlfriend Sally a laugh over the Christmas break with a bit of a slide show.

I opened the first box, unsure of its content, and started looking at the pictures. To my delight I saw almost immediately some beautiful, gentle pictures of village life and views and lovely memorable moments captured on our Sundays spent all together at Rodbourne, which took me straight back to being a child.

As I continued gradually flicking through the pictures some of them made me cry with their instant impact. I had not seen many of them before - and they stirred up wonderful memories. Some I had seen, a long, long time ago, when on Sunday nights, we used to sometimes have a slide show in the sitting room at Pound Farm. Gran used to show us all her latest pictures and we would have a supper of bread, cheese or cold meat, and home-made pickles. The grown-ups had beer or Babycham - depending on their gender! I used to love those slide shows with the running commentary from Gran but, on recollection, I think mum and dad mostly enjoyed their Babycham and beer.

The pictures continued to provoke memories of time spent at Pound Farm and when I came across a 'beauty', I allowed myself to be immersed in remembering not only the visual content of the picture but also the smells and sounds that went with the memory. It was weird, because I felt I could actually smell the kitchen with its aroma of gravy or cooking apples or fried breakfast, or the sitting room that smelt of the fireplace, with the fire either unlit and smelling of soot or lit and smelling of burning wood or coal.

If it ever rained and we were out at Pound Farm during the colder months, Martin and I had to play indoors, usually in the sitting room, as it was the warmest. I remember *feeling* the silence, except for the ticking of the grandfather clock or the fire crackling or hissing. Sometimes Gran used to allow Martin and me to make toast on a old toasting fork over the fire, which always tasted brilliant. There were always things to play with, inside or out, and when we were forced inside by the weather we used to sit drawing or crayonning pictures together, just able to hear the grown-ups in another room laughing or chattering while getting dinner or supper ready. It was a nice feeling to be left in charge of the fire and be by ourselves in our own world, but knowing that we weren't entirely alone in the house.

Because Gran didn't ever throw much out over the years, there were always lots of old annuals and toys that belonged to my mum and her brother George from when they were children and lived at Pound Farm. There was also a lovely big old dolls house that had a thatched roof and opened at the front, that once belonged to my mum. It had a few old bits of home-made dolls furniture in it and I loved playing with it. It often got dragged out on rainy days from the store room next to the kitchen, which used to be the dairy used for milking when Gran and Gramp had their cows.

There was also a marvellous old mangle in the dairy that threatened to crush your fingers if you weren't careful. Sometimes, I used to help Gran wring out her washing. I used to love the grown-up danger of it and loved the smell of the clean washing. I used to be amazed at the different coloured water from each garment falling into the basin below. I suppose that mangle got thrown away when they moved.

Something that Gran did give me at the same time as she gave me the old photo albums in 1976, was a pile of about a hundred 1950s *Eagle* comics, some still in very good condition. These, among stacks of old *Woman's Weeklys* and other magazines, were always kept - seemingly unread - tied up with string in the dairy. I still have them today.

It was always very exciting if Martin and I were allowed to stay at Gran's for some time in the summer holidays - without my mum and dad. One memory I have from when I was about five years old, is waking up quite early in a huge double bed - which felt like it had at least four eiderdowns and various blankets put on it - after having had an excitable night of playing games, listening to the trains or the owl outside and using the po kept under the bed. The po obviously amused us a lot as we had a proper toilet at home. Gran and Gramp had an outside bucket lavatory and just one cold tap downstairs until the day they moved out in 1976. As children, we thought it was all marvellous - like camping - but to live with every day it must have been a lot of work and at times very difficult.

Usually on hearing us wake, my Gran would bring up a china jug and bowl, with the jug full of warm water for washing which she set down on the old dresser. That's one of the other smells I remember - soap, and a slightly damp towel smell where Gran or Gramp had used the towel earlier on. We were then expected to get up and wash and get dressed. Meanwhile, the waft of bacon and eggs was creeping up the staircase, tempting us down.

One particular morning we were awake before Gran and Gramp and we crept in our night clothes into their bedroom next door. They were just waking. I remember them making us laugh - putting in their false teeth and making funny faces and giving us sips of tea from a flask by Gran's bedside. We jumped into their bed for a cuddle and started chattering away. I remember making them both cry with laughter by earnestly telling them, among other things, that dad had told me that he flew Wellington bomber planes in the Second World War and had been very brave. I'm sure that my dad never did tell me this and I just made it up for reasons only a six year old would know. Besides, he was only a boy during the war.

During my childhood, the Second World War was still talked about a lot and was by no means forgotten. I used to love watching 'All our Yesterdays' on the TV and I've got extracts in one of my old school diaries saying that mum and dad allowed Martin and me to watch 'The Winston Churchill Show'(!?) as a treat.

So many of Gran's pictures visually provoked memories of outdoor smells which were particularly in abundance in the autumn. The smell of ripened plums, apples and blackberries. The smell of mushrooms and fungus in the woods when we would take a walk on Sunday afternoons. The smell of woodsmoke from outside, which smelt so differently inside the house.

It's strange how looking at the pictures brought all of this and more, flooding back and how I enjoyed basking in it.

Even now, when I look at the colour pictures I've chosen for the book, it's easy to be transported back. I hope other people reading the book will be transported back to their own memories too.

During the search, I found pictures of other local villages, events and locations. I also found plenty of embarrassing pictures of Martin and myself but, fortunately for us, my original slide show idea seemed to fade as I found more and more beautiful pictures of Pound Farm and Rodbourne.

I remember starting my tentative viewing early afternoon, and not surfacing until early evening, only too aware of remaining hundreds of 'yet to be viewed' transparencies. I realised that there was no going back, and that this journey into my emotions and childhood could only be finished by looking at every single picture. So I did. It took me three days, I got several headaches and a bit of eye strain as a result of looking into the tiny viewer, but I did it.

While going through them, I kept aside any that I really liked in a separate pile and, when I'd finished, I looked at that pile again and again. I managed to edit it down to a definitive selection, most of which you will see in this book. Being a graphic designer, working with images and photographers regularly, helped me to instinctively choose those images which were not only beautiful pictures, but which also held a special importance to me personally. At this time, producing a book was the furthest thought from my mind.

I showed the edited pictures to various people I felt would enjoy looking at them, including my friend Colette Blanchard, who instantly loved them. She said that they unexpectedly made her feel very emotional too. She loved them for the way that they captured the English countryside, and said that I was very lucky to have had such a wonderful childhood, and how she wished she could have memories like these.

This, along with other people's favourable reactions, proved to me that the pictures did seem to have a certain power, which could provoke strong feelings in others. Usually on seeing the pictures people mourned, misty eyed, for their lost childhood. Or fondly remembered family holidays spent in the English countryside, when the sun always seemed to shine and they didn't spend hours on a motorway to get to their chosen destination, because motorways hadn't been built. Pondering on these reactions, I decided to be brave with an idea and ask Gran if I could use some of the images from the original four old black and white albums and the edited colour transparencies to approach a publisher to try and see if, together, we could do a book. At that stage I wasn't sure exactly how the book should be, but I knew that the collection of pictures had a powerful appeal.

Gran's natural ability to see things that pleased her wherever she went, and her instinct and constant desire to record these things - whether it was a view with a certain light quality, some flowers in bloom in the summer, or husband Charlie at harvesting time - fascinated me. To me, this was such a simple, pleasing notion, and I saw in her the pure instinct of a natural photographer. Also, the fact that she had belonged to the Kodak Fellowship Club back in the 1920s and learnt some good, basic composition and lighting skills assisted her to carry on taking well constructed pictures all her life.

Her ability to see beauty in simple things was very much encouraged in our family and strongly instilled in us all as children. I am very glad of this, as without this simple ability I would not have had the desire to even begin such a project, nor would I have have seen the importance of producing this book.

It was also interesting to me that over the three years that it took to develop the book (and to get a publishing deal!) lots of people involved along the way had their own vision of it. Some of them wanted the words to be the book - with the pictures supporting the words, as Gran's memory is so fantastic and her personality so special. Some wanted it just to contain the black and white images, or some just the colour transparencies, all depending on their age and interests. I always strongly maintained that it should be a natural alliance of words and pictures, both black and white and the later colour work, designed in such a way that it had the personal, cosy feel of opening a family snaps album with Gran talking you through the pictures. Because some of these pictures are also personal to me, I wanted the book to reflect my own childhood.

I was born in 1959 on the tail-end of a world that, during the 1960s, was to change forever. Had I been born some five years later I may not have been inspired to produce the book at all. I feel very lucky that I have been able to 'see' the pictures, maybe as Gran does, because I understand what they are about. I have also found it very rewarding to work with Gran, her pictures, memories and wonderful outlook on life and the eloquence with which she relays it all, in words as well as pictures.

Over the years Gran didn't deliberately try and catalogue the world around her, nor did she think that her pictures would be of particular interest or importance to anyone else in the future. She knew that she could take a good picture and she enjoyed looking at the results, as did friends and family, but I know that she never dreamed that she would one day have enough material to be used for a book. So we would both encourage people to take pictures of their lives, no matter how ordinary they feel those lives are, as they will provide future generations with so much information. It seems that family photographs are an underestimated and, sadly, often under-valued way of showing our past and local history.

I hope very much that other people will get as much pleasure from this book as Gran and I have had in doing it. I also hope that it will stir up memories and emotions in people of all ages, and maybe encourage them to look into their own family photo albums.

PHOTOGRAPH: MARTIN HAGGERTY

My various cameras have been amongst my most
precious possessions and have helped me to
capture for ever the life that was special to us.
No-one need look for the Rodbourne of my time
because it no longer exists. Life today is so
completely different, and now, at eighty years old,
I am lucky to have my memories and pictures of
how it all used to be.

GROWING UP IN MALMESBURY

I was born in Malmesbury on Whit Sunday in May 1913, so my mother used to call me Whit Sunday's child. My parents, Richard and Sarah Boulton, ran a demanding bakery and grocery business and I was the fourth of six children - two boys and four girls. Joseph was the eldest, followed by Elsie, then Fred, myself and twins, Hilda and Ruby.

Joseph died when he was only three months old. My sister, Ruby, died just before her second birthday. Her death was the result of the 1918 flu epidemic, and mother bought a big, soft doll to put near Hilda who missed her twin very badly.

When there was a death in the family everyone wore black for six months. To make this less expensive, men wore black armbands on their suits and overcoats, or had a black diamond stitched to a sleeve. Handkerchiefs and stationery had a black border and 'In Memoriam' cards were sent to friends and relatives. I remember my sister's to this day. It had an angel and a cross on the front and a religious verse inside with her birth date and death. Mother had quite a collection of these.

Mother had a black and white checked dress with black lace made for me, and we set off for the funeral in a horse-drawn carriage - the little white coffin resting across my parents' laps. As with all deaths, blinds were drawn at the windows and not lifted until the carriage left the street. Most neighbours kept theirs drawn as a mark of sympathy.

I started at Miss Thomas' infants school when I was four. She lived with her elderly mother in Bath, and arrived by train every Monday with her bicycle in the guard's van. I think she was about fifty years old and always dressed in a white blouse and long, thick skirt. She wore pince-nez and knotted her hair in a bun on top of her head.

To me, she was a wonderful, kind person, and I loved school. Our classroom was above the 'big boys' school. When the boys left Miss Thomas's they moved downstairs. The girls, at the age of six, transferred to Cross Hayes Girls' School where, aged eleven, they took the entrance exam to the Grammar School. I must have been quite bright because I took the exam at ten and passed.

The 'O' Brownie, my first camera, bought for 12s. 6d with birthday money and savings from working in the bakery and running errands.

When I started with Miss Thomas we were given trays of about a foot square barely covered in sand, and a pointed stick to draw our alphabet and numbers. To make a fresh start, we just gave the tray a gentle shake to clear it. From that we progressed to slates, slate pencils (pieces of slate shaped like a pencil) and damp cloths for cleaning. If the pencil wasn't held correctly, the awful screech that resulted set our teeth on edge. I was glad to get to the top of the class and start with paper and pencil and later paper and ink.

School was always cold. There was just one tortoise (big, round iron stove) at the end of the room and, unless the teacher kept it well stoked, those farthest from the fire really suffered. The poor children who came from the workhouse were allowed to sit near the stove as they always looked pale and thin.

We were lucky. Mother always kept us warmly dressed in hand-knitted woollens, stays like corrugated cardboard and navy blue pleated serge skirts. When Liberty bodices came out (which were fleecy lined) we wore them instead of the stays. We also wore red crocheted woollen petticoats and navy fleecy lined bloomers. We had black woollen stockings kept up by elastic garters, and black or brown soft leather boots. I hated the boots but mother insisted, saying they would keep our ankles slim. This did not follow!

To keep germs away, we wore iodine lockets, which smelt like a hospital surgery. At the slightest sign of a cold, mother rubbed our chests with camphorated oil and for a sore throat, a stocking filled with warmed bran was pinned around our necks at bedtime.

Mother always thought our insides should be as clean as our outsides, so every Friday was syrup of figs night. It got so that just the mention of the word would make me feel sick. Oh, the agonies the next morning - the tummy ache and the frequent dashes to the lavatory! This was situated at the

**Cross Hayes Girls' School, Malmesbury, 1921.
I am fourth from right in the front row.**

end of a long yard, past the bakehouse, stable, brewhouse and cart shed. If Polly, the carthorse, had her head over the stable door I thought she would jump over and attack me so I would stand and scream until someone came to take me past. Poor Polly didn't have a jump in her - she had peacefully pulled the bread cart for years - but that didn't make my agitated journey any easier.

There were seasons for our childhood games. In summer it was whip and top - we used to colour the tops to see who could make the prettiest patterns - and skipping to the tune of 'Salt, Vinegar, Cayenne, Pepper'. In winter we ran with our hoops. The girls had wooden ones with sticks, the boys had metal hoops with 'U' shaped metal sticks. Then there was marbles, dibs (or five stones) and cigarette cards.

Of course, all these games were played in the street. There wasn't the crazy traffic of today, only the horse-drawn carts of the coalman, milkman, baker, butcher and travelling oil and crockery sellers. Most homes were lit by oil lamps or candles.

Hilda and I went to the church Sunday school in the morning and afternoon and often went to church again in the evening with our parents. For regular attenders, there was a party with presents at Christmas, and picnic teas in the summer.

Two farm wagons pulled by shire horses would collect the children for the picnic, which was held in a field at the edge of Malmesbury. The ladies from the church dispensed tea from steaming urns, or there was a choice of lemonade - and everybody had to remember to bring a cup.

We didn't bother with plates. We held our fish paste sandwiches in one hand and wedge of fruit cake in the other. The men of the church fixed swings in the trees and, oh, the excitement of standing in the queue waiting for your turn! The vicar was in charge of the races. Mother used to give him a 7lb tin of fruit drops and the winners each received a handful.

We had best clothes which were only worn on Sundays. One set for winter and another for summer. We had navy fleecy lined bloomers in winter and white cotton knickers in summer. An old spinster lady used to crochet the lace for the legs of our white knickers and mother always had it so it just showed below the hem of our summer dresses. I used to hate it and beg her to shorten it as the boys used to tease me at Sunday school.

Sex was a word that was never heard. When I asked mother where babies came from, she just said: "God", and I believed her. At 16, I got a terrible shock when my sister-in-law, Doris, told me the truth.

Mother was a lovely, kind person, but my father was a tyrant. There wasn't much laughter or singing when he was around. By the age of nine or ten, he had me working in the bakery during my lunch hour from school. Brother Fred and sister Elsie were already working for him. In the bakehouse, my father would lift the loaves of bread from the brick oven with a pael (wooden shovel on the end of a long wooden stick). My job was to don mittens made from old sacking, take the hot loaves from the pael and stack them around the bakehouse to cool. In the afternoons when I got home from school, I had to load the cooled bread into the delivery van. When Hilda was old enough she had to help as well.

We didn't have so much time for games after that. But a girl I was friendly with at school left to work at a photographer's shop in Malmesbury and used to lend me her Kodak Magazine to read. It made me determined to get my own camera, so I could capture some of the beauty I saw around me and keep it for myself. My pictures were always peaceful, in contrast to the harsh life I was living. I saved up birthday money and other treats until I had enough to buy a Kodak Box Brownie at the age of 12. My first picture was of Hilda holding a kitten, taken in 1925, but affording the film and developing was difficult so I had to be sparing with my pictures in those days.

Elsie ran away from home and got married just as soon as she could because she couldn't stand life with my father. Then, sadly, mother died when she had just passed 50 and I was 16. As Elsie was gone, Hilda and I had to leave school to take mother's place in the house and business. We had to grow up quickly and take on a life of even harder work.

Around this time I started helping Fred

This hymn and prayer book set were given to me in 1927 as a prize for regular attendance and good behavior at Sunday school.

My very first picture, sister Hilda holding a kitten, taken in 1925.

with the bread deliveries. Before long, I knew every house and every person in Malmesbury. We also used to deliver to the outlying villages, and that's when I first saw Rodbourne and fell in love with it. Near the bakery, I used to watch as some of the neighbours took their old prams to go wooding (collecting fallen branches for firewood). Oh, how I envied them their trips to the country - I longed to live there and on Thursday afternoons, our half day, Hilda and I would cycle into the countryside for picnics.

Through my bread deliveries I became friends with sisters Lucy and Matty who lived at Parsloe Farm in Rodbourne and Hilda and I would often meet up with them and we would all picnic together. We did have fun.

Fred was a good brother, and I enjoyed doing the rounds with him. He had been married to Doris for some time but still worked at the bakery. Until the day he vanished, that is.

He set off on his delivery round as usual, together with his workmate, John. We thought nothing of it when John returned with the money bag but no Fred. He told us Fred had stopped off to tend his potato crop. It wasn't until neighbours who lived near Fred and Doris turned up that night to ask my father where Fred was, that we realised something was wrong.

It turned out that Fred, like Elsie, simply couldn't take any more. The woman he ran off with eventually wrote to dad, saying: "Don't bother to look for us because you won't find us." We never heard from Fred again.

18

This picture was the result of a photographic hint in the Kodak Magazine. The article advised readers always to look for a natural frame for a picture. I tried out this self portrait by the Bushey Close railway arch in 1933. It had three spans - this one, the central one which crossed the Rodbourne to Startley road, and the third one which crossed the field and embankment beyond.

Hilda and I used to take trips to Rodbourne on Thursday afternoons in spring when the railway banks were covered in primroses. We always used to marvel at the strength of these bridges and the way they could take the weight of a steam engine and carriages travelling at great speed.

I remember my brother bringing Bill home in the
bakery van as a present for my birthday. Bill was a dear
friend. I used to take him on our picnics to Angrove and
Kingsmead in the large basket on the front of my sit-up-
and-beg bike. Hilda took this picture of Bill and me
outside the family bakehouse in Malmesbury in 1932.

By the age of 16, I'd got into the habit of taking my 'O' Brownie with me wherever I went. This self portrait was taken in the fields at Badminton Park in 1930. Through the Kodak Fellowship Club, I made some dear pen friends in India and Africa and we would write to each other regularly and swap photographs. My friend in India was with the RAF and his father worked on the Darjeeling Himalayan Railways. He sent me a beautiful flowered shawl, and an exquisite tea service which I have to this day.

Reggie Trott was one of my cousins from Bristol, who used to have holidays in Malmesbury with our gran (mother's mother). He used to get bored being on his own and come down to the bakery to see Hilda and me. We dressed him up in a baker boy's outfit especially for this picture.

LIFE AT THE BAKERY

Our day in the bakery started when father called us at 5.30am, and Hilda and I divided our chores between us. One would light the fire, make the tea and take it to the men in the bakehouse, the other would start the housework. After breakfast, Hilda would help with making the dough and moulding the loaves while I would look after the shop. At lunchtime we'd have to cook as well as get the van loaded for the afternoon deliveries. Afternoons were devoted to specific jobs. Mondays, Hilda and I scrubbed the bakehouse and worktops, Tuesday was flour weighing day. Father would let the flour down from the loft through a calico sleeve and one of us would turn the handle on the container that brushed and sieved it. Then we'd weigh it and put it into bags - 1-¾lb for plain flour, 1-½lb for self-raising. The bags were folded, and the tops turned in, then patted flat for packing. Wednesday, one of us tended the shop while the other helped with the cake making. In those days, fresh eggs were only available in summer and we got them from farmers - who couldn't afford to pay us - in lieu of money for their bread. We preserved the eggs in barrels of water glass in the brewhouse, and it was a miserable job in winter time to have to plunge your arm into the freezing water to retrieve them. They had to be cracked separately in case one was bad, then whipped ready to go in the cake mixture. The big, round tins had to be lined with

In the depression of the 1930s there were lots of miners out of work, and other unemployed, who would travel from town to town singing or playing instruments on street corners to earn a bit of money. This man dressed as Charlie Chaplin to get more attention and the children were fascinated by him.

greaseproof paper, then all the fruit and cherries weighed. Thursday afternoon was supposed to be half day, but if Hilda and I didn't scoot through our chores in time, we'd end up having to weigh out everything in the shop and keep customers waiting. It was all weighed separately then - butter was sliced into 2oz, 4oz or 8oz slabs, then wrapped in a greaseproof paper parcel. Soda, sugar, tea - one weighed while the other packed. Friday we were busy in the shop all day as everyone used to stock up for the weekend. Saturdays, we were up at 2.30am because we had to bake all night to make up for not baking on Sundays. Hilda and I would make a big roast lunch on Sundays and father would bake other people's meat for a penny. Then it would be time to catch up on the weekly book-keeping and accounts. We

had two young men, Bill Thornbury and John Taylor, who helped out. John used to live in Rodbourne and, when he left school, he went to work in the brick yard there for ten shillings a week. When brother Fred decided we needed help, he suggested John come to us and my father paid him fourteen shillings a week. His mother called him at 3.30am every morning and he cycled into Malmesbury. There were no battery lamps in those days and he said he just had to guess where he was going in the dark! He and Bill helped in the bakehouse and with the delivery rounds. The only light in the bakehouse was a little oil lamp hung on the wall. In winter, even with the lamp, it was dark and when the lamp smoked the men could barely see. It used to get so hot in there that Fred would sometimes faint.

How well I remember that dress! It was mushroom coloured satin with a cream georgette collar, tie and cuffs trimmed with cream lace. I was window shopping in Cirencester with Hilda and my sister-in-law, Doris, and I fell in love with it. We all trooped into the shop, I tried the dress on and it felt very grand. It cost 12s.6d. It doesn't sound much today but that was my week's wages in 1933. I didn't have any money so Doris offered to lend it to me. I came out of the shop on cloud nine and rushed home to find mum and tell her of my wonderful buy. I had to pay Doris back in two instalments. Sadly, mum died soon after this and never saw me wearing my lovely dress.

My friend, Margaret Ponting, helped me take this shot by her drawing room window so I could try out my new portrait attachment lens. Nervously, we put my 'O' Brownie on books on a table opposite me, looked through the view finder to make sure we'd got it right, then she opened the shutter, counted a few seconds, then closed the shutter. It was difficult to see through the view finder because in those days it was like looking through frosted glass! There were only eight frames on a film so it didn't take long to use up. Then, like two excited adventurers, we got it printed. It cost 1s.10d to get a roll of film developed, and we were more than thrilled with the results.

Left: This was a self-portrait, taken on one of our early picnics at Angrove. I'd been swimming and my hair is loose to dry. It wasn't done to walk about with your hair like that, of course, so I had to pin it up again before I went home. I took the picture by standing the camera to face me, and tying a piece of string to the shutter. When I was ready, I pulled it.

Below: When you joined the Kodak Fellowship Club, you were sent a certificate to keep. Through my pen friends in the Club who lived abroad, I got to learn a lot about the world, which fascinated me because in those days foreign travel was not commonplace, as it is now.

Left: My schoolfriend, Cathy, used to work at the photography shop in town run by Mr Basevi. Through her, I got to know him and he used to get me to model for him. He'd make cardboard cut-outs of the pictures and stand them in the shop window to advertise his business. He didn't pay me but I enjoyed doing it as a change from the drudgery at home.

FAMILY OUTINGS

Before she died, mother worked hard in the grocery shop and was determined to enjoy life a little, so bought an old Chevrolet car. It had room for two in front and three in the back plus two small tip-up seats. It had originally belonged to Stuart Cole, the local garage owner, and had been used for taxi work - hence the extra seating.

Mother used to get the books done on a Sunday morning and pack a lovely picnic tea and off we would go - much to granny's disgust. She would give us dire warnings that the Sabbath was only meant for going to chapel and reading religious books. Dad didn't always come with us - more often than not, he'd get into one of his tempers and stomp off to bed with a glass of whisky instead.

Savernake Forest (below left) was one of mother's favourite spots. There's Fred relaxing with a mouthful of cake, with his wife Doris, clutching her cup of tea, on one side and Hilda on the other. We did enjoy those trips.

Another family favourite was a visit to Evesham (right), where we'd hire a boat and be taken up the river to Evenlode. Dad did his bakery training at Tewkesbury, which was nearby, and liked to go back and visit some of his old haunts.

Mother also bought Hilda and me second-hand bicycles at thirty shillings each. We learned to ride in the Horsefair, where an elderly man, who had lost a leg in the First World War, used to hire out bikes and teach children how to master them. If we could get our chores done quickly on a Thursday, we'd take the afternoon to cycle out.

This is Hilda at Malmesbury Common (above left), taken on one of those trips. We thought going to Malmesbury Common was like getting to the end of the world - people travelled so little then. It was very quiet down there but had a road, First Road, that was one and a quarter miles long and completely straight - perfect for cycling. Those bikes gave us so much pleasure. Hilda's wearing a black and white herringbone pattern dress - I had the same thing in navy and white - which we got just after mother died.

From left, brother Fred, sister Hilda, sister-in-law Doris, mum and dad on a trip to Evesham in 1928.

I enjoyed taking pictures of different and unusual things and I was very interested in the history of Malmesbury. Snow never used to stay very long in the town, so when it appeared, I thought it would be a good opportunity to take pictures of the three main things of historical interest in Malmesbury with their unfamiliar dusting of white. I had to deliver some bread so took my camera with me and took these photographs while out on the round.

Left: The market cross, below left: the Abbey, below: the steeple, Malmesbury.

John Taylor was one of the young men who used to work at the bakery. One of his jobs was to collect the coal every morning to feed the oven. Dad would buy a train waggon load of coal and keep it at the bottom of the garden, where John went to fetch it in an old wheelbarrow. In winter, he had to clear the path of snow before he could make his journey.

Those were the days! Through our bread deliveries, we had got to know most of the families in Rodbourne and were especially friendly with Charlie's sisters, Lucy and Matty, from Parsloe Farm. Whenever they invited us out for a picnic, Hilda and I would bolt our chores and use our half day on Thursdays to cycle out to join them. Lucy and Dorothy Greenhill (later to become Dorothy Payne) would provide the picnic, I'd bring my portable wind-up gramophone and we'd walk from Rodbourne, down through Angrove Wood and across the fields to Kingsmead Mill. Once we'd settled ourselves, we'd don our long, black bathing suits and go for a swim in the cold water. Then we felt we deserved our picnic.

From left: That's Hilda in the black beret on the left, Lucy - carrying my gramophone - centre, and Doreen Love, also wearing a beret, on the right, walking through Angrove Wood to the picnic. Berets were all the rage. Then there's the gang relaxing before a swim, clockwise from left: Flo Beecham, Lucy, Dorothy Greenhill, her sister Isabel, myself (hidden), Hilda and Joan Barton. Matty took the picture. Next, the girls getting dressed after bathing and then myself with the car inner-tube that kept me afloat - I couldn't swim. And finally, me drying my face, Hilda with hands on hips and Isabel on the right drying her legs.

I made this bag from a kit that was advertised in a magazine. It was great fun to make and only cost a few shillings. I worked the tapestry in two parts which I joined together and sewed to the frame, then lined it with rose pink material. I made it over 60 years ago and it brings back many happy memories of when I was courting Charlie and the dances we used to go to. I used it to carry my dance programme, comb, lipstick and my book of powder leaves - which we all used, as compressed powder hadn't been invented.

COURTING CHARLIE

I first met Charlie on one of the bread deliveries to Parsloe Farm when I was about 14. I thought he had a lovely face, and he was so kind. Our families became quite close - Hilda and I with his sisters, Lucy and Matty, and mother with his parents, so we visited the farm quite regularly.

After the picnics, Hilda and I would often stay to tea and Charlie, who had been working on the farm all day, would join us. We always got on well but he had another girlfriend at the time, so I didn't hold out much hope. I had my fair share of boys interested in me, many of whom I'd known from school, and they'd take me out for walks or bike rides. Mother was quite strict where boys were concerned, so I never went to dances with them or anything like that.

Then one year, at the Malmesbury Carnival, Charlie bumped into my sister and said: "Hello Hilda, where's Vera?" He found me, and asked if I wanted to go on the rides with him. We tried out all the amusements and had a wonderful time. After that, he used to come and see me twice a week. We'd take my dog, Bill, for walks or go to the cinema in Malmesbury. He had an old Austin Seven car, so sometimes we'd go into Chippenham to the pictures. I thought Lillian Gish was wonderful and watching those films was like stepping into another world.

In those days, there were also lots of parties, with formal, written invitations requiring a written reply. The Hospital, Bowls Club, Conservative Association and Young Farmers all held regular dances. Everybody wore evening dress and I made my own evening bag out of tapestry. At the dances, as you went in, the girls were given small cards folded like books with a pencil on a string, and the men had to book them for a certain dance. Charlie always booked most of mine - we loved dancing. Some of our favourite songs were 'Pasadena', 'I'll Be Loving You, Always' and 'Monterey'.

Hilda was courting George Murray, who was a school teacher in Malmesbury, and we used to make up a foursome. Before Charlie got his car, Lucy and Matty would cycle to the dances - their evening dresses tied up round their waists under their winter coats!

Charlie didn't so much propose as suggest that, as his parents had the chance to get Pound Farm, we should get married and go and live there. Did I agree? I thought it was a wonderful idea, and said so. He was busy with the haymaking at the time, so I went to a jeweller we knew and took five rings to Rodbourne so we could choose one together. We kept our engagement secret until I had the ring on my finger.

Charlie said he'd ask my father for my hand but I told him to leave dad to me. It was just as well, because father wasn't at all keen on the idea of me getting married. In fact, his first words were: "But what am I going to do?" I said he'd have to find someone else to work in the bakery because I had no intention of giving up Charlie.

My second camera, a No 2 Brownie. I bought it because it gave me a larger image than my 'O' Brownie.

This is Parsloe Farm where Charlie lived with his parents, and sisters Lucy and Matty. It was taken in the early summer of 1937, the year we got married. That May, it was the jubilee of King George V and Queen Mary and everybody decorated their houses with flags. I still hadn't moved to Rodbourne by then, but the village held a celebratory party and huge picnic.

If a sow in Rodbourne gave birth to more piglets than she had teats for, the 'tiddlers' would be given to Lucy and Matty. If the weaklings survived and could be fattened up, it meant extra cash for the family. This is Charlie with one of the tiddlers in front of the brewhouse at Parsloe Farm in 1936.

Here's Charlie with his parents' dog, Darkie, and the tiddler pig.
You can see it was a Sunday because Charlie's wearing a suit. It
was the custom to dress up on Sundays then - though I like to
think he put it on in my honour!

This is Hilda and Darkie outside Parsloe Farm. We'd been invited over for tea. She's wearing a shocking pink top edged with dark brown velvet collar and cuffs. I had an identical one - we often dressed alike then. We also had a brown and white checked suit each. We found the patterns, then got a dressmaker to make them up for us. The beautiful white daisies growing over the wall had a lovely grey foliage and I have some, taken from a cutting, still growing in my garden today.

Charlie and I were married in Malmesbury Abbey on September 16, 1937. I was twenty four and he was twenty six. Hilda and I did all the preparations between us, and my father baked the cake and paid for the reception. I had five bridesmaids - Lucy and Matty, Hilda, my school-friend Margaret Ponting, and my six-year-old niece Glenna.

The four older bridesmaids wore green dresses, trimmed with dark green velvet, and held bouquets of pink carnations and mauve scabias. Glenna's dress was a mass of rose coloured frills and she had a small posy of the same flowers. I chose the pattern for my dress and had it made up by the court dressmaker, Maud Brooks, in Cirencester. It was cream cloquét with net backing and had an Elizabethan collar, with sleeves puffed to the elbow then tightly fitting to the wrist with tiny buttons running from elbow to wrist. It also had a built-in train. I carried a shower bouquet of white carnations, white stephanotis and lots of fern. Charlie and I had gone to Humphries Nursery in Langley Barrell to choose the flowers, and they arrived on my wedding morning packed in a beautiful wicker hamper.

We had our reception in the Parish Hall in Malmesbury. There were around a hundred guests and we all sat down to a delicious meal of hams, salads and trifles. Hilda was courting George Murray (whom she later married), and his brother, Stan, played the violin beautifully at the reception. My father wasn't used to such large gatherings and felt too shy to make a speech, so he asked the curate to speak on his behalf. I'll always remember his words because he started with: "May bad luck always follow you..." and I wondered

what on earth was coming next! However, he went on "...but never catch you up." I breathed a sigh of relief. At my wedding, father met a widowed aunt of Charlie's, who he'd known twenty years before and not seen since. Unknown to us, he began writing to her, and they eventually got married several years later one Sunday morning at 8am in Rodbourne Church. The wedding ceremony was private, but I walked up there to take some photographs for posterity. Father sold the bakery business after I got married, and retired. He still owned thirteen houses and five lock-up garages in Malmesbury, so he didn't go hungry!

Charlie and I had a two-week honeymoon in Weymouth - the first real holiday of his life. We had a wonderful time, going for long walks along the front and taking coach trips to see the local sights. And everywhere we went we heard the latest song, 'Sweet September In The Rain', playing. I can't hear it now without thinking of those happy days.

Then it was time to return home - to Pound Farm. I just couldn't get there fast enough, knowing I didn't have to go back to the hard drudgery of the bakery - even though life on a small farm wasn't easy.

Rodbourne was the village of my dreams. When I moved there, it consisted of about twenty-two dwellings and was my idea of an old-fashioned village - the inhabitants were always ready to help each other. The whole of Rodbourne belonged to Sir John Pollen and the farmers rented their land and homes from him. They had to take their rent to the estate agent in the village school but, when the school closed down in the 1950s, we all had to queue at the kitchen door of Sir John's house and wait our turn to pay. Charlie's mother used to work for the Pollens, so when Pound Farm became vacant, she put in a good word for us and got it for Charlie. We lived at Pound Farm for forty years and were very happy there.

The house was in a very poor state when we first looked over it but I was not dismayed. It had plenty of possibilities and, as the estate had agreed to decorate to my wishes, I could visualise how it would look. The farm work was too much for one man alone but there wasn't enough money coming in to pay for another, so the extra work fell to me. I didn't mind as I enjoyed the outdoor life and Charlie and I were happy working together.

For the first few years, Pound Farm was run in conjunction with Parsloe Farm, which was run by Charlie's parents. From them, Charlie received a wage of thirty shillings a week and out of it I paid him 'pocket money' to go to the Plough Inn on a Saturday night for a game of darts and half a pint of beer - then, about 6d a pint. Later, his wage rose to £2 a week.

Luckily there wasn't much to buy as we produced most of the things we needed. The baker called three times a week and the butcher called on Friday. I kept the joint in a meat safe in the cool dairy and I used every morsel, mincing the last bit to make rissoles or shepherd's pie. When the joint was finished, we had home-cured bacon and ham, chicken and wild rabbit. I had never tasted rabbit before I met Charlie - my parents would never cook it. When the war came, wild rabbits made a very useful addition to our diet.

When I knew I was getting married, I joined the Dairy Students to learn how to deal with the practicalities of being a farmer's wife. Such as, how to pluck poultry and remove the innards in one clean movement, how to make use of every morsel of a slaughtered pig - from its head to its trotters - how to preserve and bottle fruit, and so on. I wanted to be prepared for my new life and be a help, not a hindrance, to Charlie.

In the early summer, I used to buy green walnuts from another farmer to pickle in vinegar. This had to be done before the shells formed. I would sit at the box of green nuts and stab each one several times with a fine knitting needle so that the salt and vinegar could penetrate. A dark stain would ooze from the nuts and turn my hands brown. I also used to do large sweet jars of pickled eggs. During the war, we collected rose hips which went to a factory for making rose hip syrup, which was given to children to boost their vitamins.

I also used to hatch turkeys for Christmas. Once, in Chippenham market, I bought a sitting of guinea fowl eggs and, as a hen had gone broody in the manger in the stable, I put the eggs under her. One night, when they were near to hatching, Charlie forgot to shut the stable door and a fox got in and made off with the hen. Some of the baby guinea fowl had hatched so I brought them indoors in a box of hay and put them by the kitchen range to keep warm. Only two survived and, when old enough to be let outside, would run with the hens and ducks but always roosted at night in the greengage tree.

I made 'boisters' or 'beastings' pudding from the second milking after a cow had calved. I put the milk, some sugar and a sprinkling of nutmeg in a large dish and popped it in the oven. When cooked, it was like egg custard.

In those days, several milking herds were brought through Rodbourne on their way to pasture. Lots of wild garlic grew on the grass verges and the farmers tried to eradicate it because if the cows ate too much it would taint their milk. The same applied to turnips, so the cows were only fed sparingly. Some of the farms had what was called 'three hole' lavatories - one for father, one for mother, and a small one for the children. There was no running water.

Most places had a well or shared one with a neighbour. I used to hate having to lean over the open well to fix the bucket onto the wire rope, let it down, then wind the heavy bucket back up and carry it across to the house. If the well went dry, we had to take barrels and churns in a cart to the village 'reservoir'. The water was housed in a big tank in a farmer's cowshed - fed from a spring in a field - and came out through a pipe in the wall. A chain hung by the pipe, which had to be pulled to get the water. It was amazing how much water was needed to fill the copper and get it hot enough to wash milking utensils or the family clothes. Having a bath was a great luxury, though it meant standing in a tub and doing the best one could. Water was laid on in the village in the 1950s - and it seemed wonderful to us.

During the winter, the Duke of Beaufort's hounds used to meet in the village. Charlie and other farmers took that as a day off and would walk miles over the fields, following the hunt. I loved walking, so used to have a day out as well. In the spring, we used to go to the hunt point-to-point race meeting at Alderton (now held at Didmarton). In those days, the hunt used to provide a wonderful hospitality tent for the farmers with free food and drink, and every winter held a dinner in Malmesbury Town Hall for the farmers. On the menu was venison pie from the deer herd at Badminton Park. Another enjoyable day out was a visit to the Bath and West Agricultural Show (now held every year at Shepton Mallet) and a coach used to do the rounds of the villages to take us there.

Life was hard and outings were rare, which is why we enjoyed them so much. But, at the time, it was the same for everyone and we considered this way of life to be normal.

Rodbourne School

I was bringing the cows home for milking one day in 1948, saw this scene and thought it a picture of peace. I so wanted to capture it on film I went straight home for my camera, came back and took it.

On the right of the picture is the old oak tree. During the war, when cattle feed was scarce, we would often go out in the village collecting acorns and horse chestnuts. We lived just around the corner from the oak tree and our ducks would love to get out there and gobble the acorns. But we had to try to stop them because it made their egg yolks dark brown and then they were unsaleable.

Opposite the tree is the school. In those days, children walked to school from Startley, Corston, Rodbourne Rail and Burnt Heath right out on Malmesbury Common. There was no sanitation. The 'lavatories' were buckets in a row of sheds in the school garden.

Springtime was lovely. May blossoms bordered the road and farther back on the wide verge were pink and white horse chestnuts. In January, the banks and grass were covered in snowdrops, later followed by primroses, bluebells, buttercups and cow parsley. The only sound very often was the buzzing of bees in the lime blossom. Unfortunately, lots of the trees have since been destroyed by gales and old age.

The schoolchildren had a natural playground amongst the trees. I used to love to sit in the garden and listen to the music when they were practising country dancing, ready for the church fête and other occasions.

This is the Church of the Holy Rood. The vicar used to live at Corston and his parish was Rodbourne, Corston and Foxley. We had a service every Sunday morning at eight o'clock, then again at 10.30am and 6.30pm alternate weeks. When I moved into Rodbourne, Charlie's mother and Sir John asked me to look after the altar. That meant dressing it for each of the church festivals - a mauve altar cloth for Lent, white for joyous occasions, green for harvest festival and so on.

The women of the church took it in turns to provide and arrange the flowers. When it was Sir John and Lady Pollen's turn I did it for them, which was a pleasure because they bought such beautiful flowers. When it was my turn I raided my garden.

For church festivals, the decorations were extra special, and the whole village joined in. After the plain purple for Lent, it was lovely to decorate for Easter. The villagers used to bring spring flowers from their gardens, and Peggy Taylor would line the window sills with moss then fill little paste pots with primroses and tuck them into the moss, so they looked like they were growing there. Sir John used to buy me lovely lilies to arrange on the altar. We lined the entrance porch with daffodils and greenery, then all was ready for the festival service which was a joy to attend.

In autumn, when all had been safely gathered in, the church would be decorated with flowers and produce brought by the villagers. A sheaf of corn stood by the altar and a big loaf, made specially for harvest festival, was placed in front. After the harvest festival Sunday service, the produce would be taken to Malmesbury hospital.

At Christmas we all decorated the church with holly, mistletoe, evergreens, chrysanthemums, candles and lots of red ribbon bows, and a beautiful Christmas tree stood by the altar. The midnight service on Christmas Eve was always packed as there was a certain magic about that service. It was lovely to walk out afterwards into the frosty, starry night and see the lantern swinging from the lychgate porch - it really did feel like Christmas.

In those days, after a baby was born, the mother was 'churched'. This meant giving thanks to God for a safe birth, then the woman was purified. Only the mother and the person who was with her when the baby was born would attend. My elder sister Elsie stayed with me when my first child, Anna, was born so she came to my churching. It was younger sister Hilda's turn at the birth of my son George.

Christenings were carried out after morning service. Everyone who attended church that morning would stay on for the christening service, but only friends and family would go to the celebratory lunch afterwards. When confirmation services were held, they were conducted by the Bishop of Bristol, and children from other dioceses came to be confirmed here. Dorothy Payne from Manor Farm and I ran the Sunday school for the village children and when they were confirmed, Sir John and Lady Pollen gave each child a prayer book with their name embossed on the cover. People from Malmesbury would come to worship in Rodbourne because they enjoyed the atmosphere of this rural church, so central to village life.

This is my friend, Margaret Ponting, flanked by Charlie on the right and his favourite cousin, Billy Dawkins, on the left. Billy was like a brother to Charlie. Margaret was an old friend from my schooldays and we used to go on holidays together before I was married. She was my bridesmaid and, now into her eighties, she's still my friend. After I got married she used to come and stay for weekends - and loved it. Sometimes, Billy would stay too, and in the evenings we would go for long walks over the fields. This was taken on one of our walks across Forty Acres in 1939.

Charlie was still working for his parents when we were first married, and I used to have to go up to Parsloe Farm to collect the milk. When Margaret stayed she used to come with me and, if we took a jug, Charlie's mother would also give us a drop of cream. We used to have it for our tea with some of the fruit we'd picked on our walks. Being a baker's daughter, I often baked my own bread and we'd have sandwiches, home-made cakes, and home-made jam. This picture was taken when I was pregnant with Anna in 1939.

The pace and cycle of life on the farm was dictated by the seasons. In spring, we would get up at six every day of the week to start the milking. The cows all knew their own places in the stalls and stood patiently waiting to be chained up. They didn't have numbers on their hind-quarters as they do today but names over their stalls - flower names, such as Daisy, Primrose or Violet.

The first two weeks of April were known as blackthorn winter. That was because the hedges looked like drifts of snow with their white blossom, and it was always very cold then. April 23, St. George's Day, was considered the ideal time to pick dandelions for wine. I also used to gather elder flowers and cowslips for wine. We had one field covered in cowslips, which was supposedly a sign of poor ground, so we'd spread it with farmyard manure kept aside for this purpose whenever the cow sheds were mucked out.

March 25 and September 29 were quarter days, when farm labourers - whose term of work had ended - moved on to another village. The farmer would usually offer the labourer the use of a big farm wagon and one or two shire horses to move his meagre belongings. Everybody was poor, farming was at a low ebb, and we only got 6d a dozen for eggs, 6-8d a gallon for milk, and a man would come round to buy wild rabbits to sell in the town. He paid us 6d per rabbit.

Summer was a busy time outdoors. When the young cattle were taken to the fields for the first time, they shrank back from the open door of the calf house, then came bolting out like mad things and jumped around. This was when good neighbours, like Frank and Jim Reynolds, came to help - one walking ahead closing any open gates and the other keeping the straying calves within the herd. Charlie brought up the rear with Toby, the faithful labrador we had as a puppy from Frank.

The milking cows stayed out overnight in summer, so every morning they had to be brought home for milking. We would get up at 5.30am, light the range to boil the kettle and have a cup of tea and a biscuit before Charlie set off on his bike to fetch the cows. This was quite a distance, as everybody in Rodbourne had a few fields near their farm while the rest were all on the outskirts of the village.

Sometimes Charlie would come back to say that someone had left the gate open and the cows had strayed into the wood. That meant I had to go and help find them. If it was a wet morning we could get soaked from the waist down pushing through the undergrowth.

When all the cows were accounted for we had to get them home as quickly as possible as the milk lorry called at 8am and the driver didn't like to be kept waiting. In those days, to cool the milk before sending it off, a tank had to be filled with water from the well. The tank was up high so the water would run down a rubber tube to the cooler. The milk went in a tank over the cooler and when the tap was turned on, the milk ran over the cooler into the churn underneath. The churn had a special sieve over the top so that the milk was properly strained.

It was a very tiring job keeping the water tank filled and lifting the big buckets of milk into the tank. The milk churns held ten gallons each and they all had to be properly measured, then labelled with the farmer's name and address and amount of milk in each churn. This all had to be done every night and every morning. We were lucky that our milk was picked up so early before the sun's heat could spoil it because it was all quality tested at the dairy and you were soon notified if yours didn't make the grade.

My job was to feed the pigs and poultry and let them out, then cook a good breakfast for Charlie. Sometimes, when collecting the cows, he'd bring home some wild mushrooms and we'd have them with our home-cured bacon and eggs. The aroma in the kitchen was wonderful. After breakfast Charlie would feed and water our old cart horse, Dreamer, then take the cows back to pasture before starting the work for that day. I had to fetch water from the well and boil it to sterilise all the milking utensils.

Dinner was always at noon and if we were going to eat at home I had to think about preparing that. After washing up, it was back to farm work. There was grass to cut and dry for haymaking, weeds to be hoed from the mangold field, thistles to be grubbed out and, before you could turn round, it was time to fetch the cows back for the afternoon milking. That was usually my job while Charlie put a little cattle cake in the manger at each cow's place. Once home, there was time for a pre-milking cup of tea before a repeat of the morning's milking programme.

Mowing the grass and stacking it ready for haymaking was hot and tiring work during the summer months and we were always glad when good weather allowed us to get it finished in record time. That meant we got a break between haymaking and harvest time and we would take a day off and go to Chippenham market. I would come back so very pleased with a pretty, cheap remnant of material to make a new cushion cover for Charlie's armchair in the kitchen. The children would be delighted with a colouring book and pack of crayons. Charlie would be happy meeting old friends and finding out what had won the 2.30 race meeting.

After haymaking, when the corn was ripe, harvesting started. When the fields had been cleared I used to go back in the evening and fill sacks with the fallen and broken heads of corn. As the children grew up they came with me. This was called gleaning, a very back-breaking job, but the poultry loved the corn.

After haymaking and harvesting, autumn was soon with us, which meant getting everything ready for winter. The long rows of potatoes in the plough field had to be dug and gathered into sacks. Charlie dug while I had another back-breaking job - picking them up. The smallest ones would be kept aside for boiling up for pig and poultry food, mixed with the meal ground at Kingsmead Mill from our corn. In the evening there were all the garden vegetables to lift and store and all the apples to pick. When I had any spare time I would make chutneys and pickles with green beans, apples, tomatoes and onions.

I enjoyed the days of autumn when I used to walk along the hedges picking blackberries and crab apples for jelly and jam, sloes and elderberries for wine. On fine Sunday afternoons we would walk through the wood gathering hazel nuts and sweet chestnuts, filling a knapsack on Charlie's back. These were supposed to be kept for Christmas but the store was often raided before then. When we were sitting before the open fire at night, the wind howling around the house,

Charlie would put some chestnuts on the coal shovel and roast them.

When I had finished making the jams, jellies, bottled fruit, pickles, chutneys and bottles of wine, my store cupboard was a picture. We also had soft fruit in the garden besides the apples, plums and pears, and I made good use of it all. In the kitchen hung hams and sides of bacon, cured and wrapped in muslin, ready for winter.

Autumn was also the time for coppicing in the wood. This meant cutting out the hazel and ash wood for making hurdles for sheep pens. This was Jim Willis' job. Attired in black bowler hat and black overcoat, he would cycle from Malmesbury to Bincome Wood accompanied by son Fred - both on their sit-up-and-beg bikes. They would take their meals and stay at work all day. Jim was paid 4d a square foot for cutting down a tree. He was the grandfather of today's Willis Bros who are the course builders for the Badminton Horse Trials. When talking to Gerald, one of Jim's four grandsons, recently, he told me they still make hurdles the way his grandfather did - without any machinery, using only hand tools.

When the clocks changed and the nights drew in we knew that winter was on its way. The cows had to be kept in during the winter months. They were turned out in the yard after milking for some exercise while their shed was cleaned and fresh straw bedding put in the stalls. Water was not laid on in the cow shed, so Charlie had to dip dozens of buckets into the pond in the field and carry it in for each cow to drink. A cow will drink several gallons so it was real hard work. During frosty weather, the ice had to be broken first.

When snow was on the ground, food had to be carted to the young cattle wintering in the fields and the ice broken on the ponds. Those were days of cold hands and feet and stinging chilblains, and we used to resort to the tin of Zambuk ointment or the ball of 'snow fire' to ease the pain.

Then the first snowdrops would start to push through the grass verges along the village lanes and we could start to look forward to spring again.

I liked to take pictures of the jobs Charlie did around the farm. This showed him chopping wood for kindling. We used to prop up the cut wood to dry by the old elm trees, and the village children would come and play 'house' in their shelter.

These pictures were taken around Kingsmead Mill - the scene of those early picnics with Charlie's sisters before I was married. It was so beautiful in the Bluebell Wood.

The Mill Pond (below) was attached to the mill. We'd walk through Angrove Wood, on through the fields then over the rickety wooden bridge to get to the mill. On the other side of the bridge was an eel trap.

After threshing in the autumn, Charlie would bring our corn to the mill to be ground into meal to feed the pigs and cattle through the winter. We would also take a walk through the fields to the mill on a Sunday evening to buy plums from the miller's wife, Mrs Bye. I would preserve some of the plums in bottles for later use, and make the others into jam and chutney.

Left: I took this further down the river towards Angrove because I loved the reflections of the trees and the buttercups in the still water.
Below: I thought this bridge, which was used by the cows and an occasional horse and cart, was beautiful. Sadly, it's no longer there.

50

In the winter we needed plenty of wood to keep the range, the boiler and the open fires stoked up. Whenever Charlie had a spare moment from farming, he'd saw up some logs and stack them to dry ready for use later. On the left is an old shepherd's settle (they used to have these in their huts) that our children later played on. You can tell that Christmas is upon us by the turkeys hanging in the trees waiting to be plucked.

Above: This is Charlie and Toby, our first dog, standing by the coal house. The coalman used to call once a fortnight and we paid 1s.10d a hundredweight. Charlie's holding a shovel and a gun and was about to go out rabbiting. This was the car Charlie had before we were married. We couldn't afford to run it once the war started because we were unable get enough petrol.

Right: We met Grace and Ken on our honeymoon in Weymouth and they used to come and visit us from their home in London. They came quite often, until war broke out, and then we lost touch with them. They enjoyed staying on the farm and were always happy to help out. This is Grace and me feeding the poultry and collecting the eggs.
Below: Ken with me and Dreamer, our old cart horse.

This is Anna in her bath by the kitchen door. I used to bath her every night and every morning, heating the water in a big saucepan. In winter this took place in front of the kitchen range where it was nice and warm. Here, it's summer, because she's by the door in the sunshine. She's about a year old.

Anna Is Born

Anna was born April 14, 1939. I only saw the doctor twice during the months I was pregnant. The first time was to make sure I was pregnant, the second was to ask him to come for the confinement. You had to pay ten shillings a visit then. During my pregnancy, work carried on as usual. I helped with the harvesting - lifting the heavy sheaves - feeding the pigs, poultry and so on.

The primroses were out when the baby was due, and I got through the fence at the bottom of the garden to go over the field and pick some. While I was out, my labour pains started but I got the flowers home and put them in water. When the doctor called round, he stood and admired them and I had to remind him of why he was there! The district nurse, who cycled round the villages on her wobbly bicycle, was also in attendance. We had to pay her thirty shillings a visit and 2s.6d for each bottle of medicine. There weren't many prescriptions given in those days, and no ante-natal or post-natal care.

After the confinement, mothers were kept in bed for ten days, so my elder sister, Elsie, came to stay and help out. After Anna was born, the district nurse called in over several days to bath the baby and Elsie looked after the house and

home. Sir John brought me a bottle of champagne and a bouquet, as we were the oldest family on the estate.

Our nearest neighbours were Kate and Jim Reynolds and their children, Frank and Olive. Kate's sister lived with them - a prim, elderly and childless widow known as Aunt Hannah. During my ten-day stay in bed, she thoughtfully brought me a lovely cooked dinner. I was sitting up in bed, the window open so that I could see across the fields, and Aunt Hannah said: "Mind you don't catch a cold in your bosoms!"

I felt so weak after staying in bed all that time but work had to carry on - babies wore long gowns for at least six weeks in those days, so I had to fetch all the water from the well to fill the boiler to wash them. Today there are classes on baby care, but then we had to do the best we could. In the September of that year, I was giving Anna her bath when Frank Reynolds looked over the hedge and told me that war had broken out. I said it wouldn't affect us in Rodbourne - little did I realise!

Anna was a happy, contented baby and she grew up loving the country life. She was always eager to go out and about on the farm with Charlie and followed him everywhere, as faithfully as his shadow.

Right: Here's Charlie and Anna with Granny the cow and her calf. Granny was the first calf Charlie's father gave him and she bore us five calves in all. She had just had this one and I wanted a picture of them. Beside Charlie is a pile of wood laid ready for chopping, and behind him is where our well stood. The well was a long walk from the house and the bucket was heavy.

Below: I bred turkeys in what we called the jailhouse - that old wooden hut in the background - that Charlie bought at a farm sale to keep cattle meal in. I'd hatch the turkeys from eggs and, the white ones in particular, were very delicate. The slightest thing could kill them off so I was proud when I reared any to maturity. At Christmas time they'd be slaughtered then strung up in the trees to drain the blood, which made the meat white. If it was too cold outside, I'd sit in front of a big old tea chest in the kitchen to pluck them. This was a mammoth task as we used sell a lot of poultry at Christmas.

When it was done, I'd sew newspaper bags (you didn't get many ready-made bags in those days) fill them with feathers and bake them in the oven to kill the fowl fleas. The feathers would go to make pillows and eiderdowns.

WORKING THE MANGOLD FIELDS

Mangolds and turnips were grown as cattle feed, and planted in spring. To do this, we used a small seed drill. Charlie took the handles at the back and it fell to me to have a rope around my middle and guide the drill, while he kept an eye on the funnel in the centre to make sure the seed was passing through. Sometimes I did not always tread the straight and narrow path and when the seedlings came through it showed. Uncle Tom used to cycle over from Seagry Heath Farm occasionally on a Sunday evening and walk around to look at the crops. One day, he commented: "The fellow who pulled that seed drill must have been drunk". I kept quiet!

As the young plants formed, it was time to thin them out. Charlie would take one row with his hoe, knocking out unwanted plants to leave the good ones room to grow. I wasn't so accurate with a hoe, so I'd do my row on my hands and knees, thinning with a kitchen knife. What a back-breaking job - I was always glad when it was lunchtime. Toby, our faithful dog, used to sit by the pram and guard Anna while we worked.

She was a happy and contented child, who delighted in going everywhere on the farm with her father. When I took this picture in 1941, Charlie and I had been hoeing the man-golds and swedes. We used to take a picnic meal as the fields were quite a way from the house. Anna is wearing her sun bonnet, as she was one of those babies born with just a coating of golden down on her head - later to become a mass of golden curls. She would be quite happy looking for wild flowers, guarded by Toby, and I captured her here amongst the moon daisies.

Over the fence in the picture is the London to Fishguard railway line. Wild strawberries grew along the banks and we would take home a basinful to have with cream for our tea. The railway bank was a wonderful place for finding lots of different kinds of wild flowers. On Sunday evenings in summer, we used to take the children there and teach them the names of the flowers. Also in summer, we used to pay thirty shillings to the Great Western Railway to cut the grass on the embankment. They were glad for us to do it because sparks from the engines used to cause grass fires. We were glad because it made extra hay for the cattle in winter. Today, with the fast trains passing through, there is a £200 fine for anyone caught walking along the banks.

If mangold thinning was back-breaking work in the spring, picking up potatoes and pulling up the mangolds was just as gruelling in autumn. We'd cut off the leaves and tap roots of the mangolds, pile them in heaps in their rows, and cover them with leaves until we could take our old horse, Dreamer, and the cart to collect them. After loading, we would bring them back to the farm yard where they would be covered in straw to store for winter feed for the cattle, then chopped as needed in an old hand turned cutter. To make the feed, the chopped vegetables would be mixed with barley meal, ground from our own corn at Kingsmead Mill.

We all took a turn with the cutter handle, including a schoolboy, John Stoneham, who used to love to help Charlie around the farm during his holidays to earn a little pocket money. He was a good and gentle lad with the cattle and we were all very fond of him. He would have made an excellent farmer but is now a builder.

Above: Here's Charlie hoeing the mangolds to thin them out so they could spread and grow through the summer, with Anna, as usual, by his side.

Below: At midday, we'd all sit down to a nice picnic lunch as it was too far to go back to the house - and how welcome was that bottle of Eiffel Tower lemonade! Charlie, like most men working in the fields, preferred a bottle of cold tea.

THE ANNUAL PIG KILLING

We had a pig killed every winter - it had to be done during the cold season because there was no refrigeration in those days. We never ate pork or watercress unless there was an 'R' in the month - because those were the cold months.

Billy Sutton, who lived on Malmesbury Common, was the man who toured the villages to do the butchering. He would arrive soon after 8am, when he had finished the milking on his own farm, with his knives and steel (used for sharpening the knives) wrapped in sacking and tied to the crossbar of his bicycle. After the kill, the carcass would be covered in straw and set alight to remove all the bristles and whiskers, then it was given a good scrub in my big washing tub.

The clean carcass was put on a trestle and carried into the dairy, where it was hung on a hook attached to a beam especially for this purpose. There, it was slit open, and all the offal was put on big meat plates ready for me to make faggots. The caul (stomach membrane), which looked rather like a lace curtain, had to be put in warm water to stretch it before it was opened out to wrap around the faggots.

I would cut up the fleck (fatty layer under the skin) and melt it down to make lard. Then I would boil the head, take the meat from a cooked chicken and rabbit, add herbs to taste, then set it all in jelly (made from boiling the trotters) to make brawn. The intestines were soaked, thoroughly washed, then turned in salt water, plaited and boiled to make chitterlings. The hams, hocks and sides were cured by rubbing them with salt, salt petre and brown sugar for several days. The rest of the meat was cut into joints and distributed amongst the villagers - who would return a joint to us when their own pig was killed.

To make the faggots, I'd take the minced offal and mix in chopped apples, onions, sage leaves and breadcrumbs, then I'd season it with herbs, a teaspoonful of sugar, a pinch of curry powder, salt and pepper. The mixture was divided and wrapped in pieces of the caul, then put on a baking tin and roasted. When I had made all the faggots, we used to invite all our village friends to an old-fashioned Wiltshire supper of faggots, peas and mashed potatoes.

Top: Billy Sutton, his steel hanging from his waist, about to set light to the straw, watched by Stuart Barton and Charlie.
Above: The clean carcass being carried to the dairy.

Above: The hole left after the Parsloe Farm bomb had been winched out safely.

Below: The bomb waiting to be taken out to Malmesbury Common and detonated.

We never could tell the difference between the warning siren and the sound for the all-clear, which caused a bit of confusion! Our shelter was the area under the stairs and we were convinced it would just splinter and fall on top of us if a bomb hit. Nevertheless, we put a mattress under there and would all huddle together when the warning sounded. There'd be Charlie, myself, Anna, and our evacuee - she was a bag of nerves and used to scream and cry all the time.

One night we heard this buzzing, whining noise outside. When Charlie looked out in the morning, there was a fin from a bomb lying on our tiles and an unexploded bomb in a neighbour's farmyard opposite. Another bomb came down at the back of Parsloe Farm, by the cow shed. Three bombs fell on Rodbourne that night but, thankfully, none went off. The bomb disposal squad swiftly removed the first two but the one at Parsloe Farm had buried itself deep in the ground.

At the time, Charlie's parents had an old deaf and dumb man working for them. He'd been with them for years so, fortunately, Charlie could understand his sign language. He came running from behind the cow shed waving his arms and pointing. Charlie, who'd gone up to Parsloe Farm to see his parents, realised what was wrong and notified the police. When the bomb disposal squad arrived, they evacuated everybody from the top end of Rodbourne, then took over Parsloe Farm for the next few days, so Charlie's parents came to stay with us at Pound Farm.

To retrieve the bomb from the deep hole it had made, the bomb disposal experts rigged up a tripod over the hole, then attached a winch rope to it to haul the bomb up. It started to wobble when it got to the top and the men were worried it would fall back down and explode. They eventually got it out without mishap and I went round to take these pictures. They warned everybody to keep their windows open, then took the bomb out to Malmesbury Common, and detonated it.

The bomb disposal squad outside Parsloe Farm.

GEORGE IS BORN

Charlie and me, with four-year-old Anna and new baby, George.

George was born May 24, 1943. He was a lovely baby weighing 8lb. In August of that year he became very ill and couldn't keep any food down. At only four months old, he went back to less than his birth weight. The doctor came and said he thought he had a chill on the kidneys. He asked Charlie to visit the surgery that evening and told him to be sure and stay with me as he didn't think the baby would live through the night - but not to tell me. So Charlie kept the distressing news to himself and the worry of it made him ill. I then had two invalids on my hands and had to get our neighbour, Bert Barton (Stuart's brother), to come and do the milking. There wasn't much change in the baby until the following Easter, and he still looked very ill.

Of course, farm work waits for no man and after Charlie recovered it was back to business as usual for both of us - even though we were worried about the baby. I would take George in his pram, with Anna running along beside us, to do my work - such as bringing the cows home for milking - while Charlie was out in the fields. Haymaking was a busy time and, after the grass was cut, it was left in long rows in the fields to dry. Then we had to turn it all by hand, using a rake. It makes me hot now to think of the hours I spent with burning cheeks and arms, and perspiration running down from under my straw hat. Once the grass was dry, we would stack it into haycocks - pointed mounds about 6ft high - to allow the rain to run off. Then it had to be carted back to the farmyard to be built into ricks. If hayricks were built with hay that was still damp it would go mouldy and the cows wouldn't eat it in winter.

George's health improved as he got older and he was well enough to start at the village school when he was five years old. Then, one day, he came home screaming with pain. Lucy took us to the new doctor, Dr Penman, and he gave George M & B tablets, as he thought he had a virus in his kidneys. After that, George started to thrive and never looked back.

Above: This is Charlie and Uncle Wilfred on the Fordson tractor I bought with part of a legacy I had been left. Uncle Wilf was one of my father's brothers. He worked in a bank in Staffordshire and, during the war, used to love to come and don his old clothes and help out and feel he was doing his bit for the war effort. In the background is our house, Pound Farm. Winter evenings, waiting for Charlie to come in from milking, I would gaze over the peaceful fields and watch the big old barn owl skimming the hedge looking for mice.

Right: This was my father's other brother, Fred Boulton. He used to come out for the day with my Aunt Nell and help out with haymaking and harvesting. Here, he's giving Charlie a hand cutting the grass to make hay.

THRESHING TIME

Towards the end of the war, we hired David Cole and his new tractor to help with the field work. At harvest time, he pulled the reaping machine, which would cut the corn and tie it into sheaves with binding twine. My job was to follow behind and stand the sheaves, heads uppermost, in stooks (stacks) of six to eight to allow the air to circulate and dry the corn. The stooks were arranged in an inverted 'V' shape so the rain would run off easily. They were left in the fields for a couple of weeks if the weather was good. When the stooks had dried, the tractor took the place of Dreamer (who had died) to pull the cart piled with corn back to the farmyard to be built into ricks. Then the corn had to be threshed, and this was done by the visiting threshing machine. This belonged to a farmer who lived in Long Newton, and he toured the countryside hiring it out to the farmers. There weren't many telephones then but word soon got round when he was due in the village and we'd work out a rota between us - everyone helping out at each farm. We were allowed extra rations of margarine, cheese and tea to feed the labourers. The threshing machine was fed with corn from the rick, and it separated the ears from the stalks, or straw, and also sifted the weeds and other rubbish. The straw was built up into another rick to be used for feed or bedding in the winter. The sacks of corn were taken to Kingsmead Mill to be ground. All this work is done by combine harvester today.

Above: The village men who came to help out at threshing time. Dick Salter is in the foreground with the terriers, then from left, the man who brought the threshing machine, my Charlie, Frank Reynolds, Stuart Barton, Jim and Charlie Reynolds, Herb Broom (back) and Bill Knott.

Left: The threshing machine in action.

Charlie in his homeguard uniform.

This picture was taken when the men had just been issued with their new uniforms and wanted to show them off.

DAD'S ARMY

The homeguard was made up with village men from neighbouring areas and Jim Reynolds, John Baker, Frank Reynolds and Charlie were amongst those from Rodbourne. They were called the LDV - Land Defence Volunteers. They were issued with khaki uniforms and rifles but no ammunition.

Being countrymen, they all owned shotguns, so used the cartridges with the shot emptied out to produce satisfying, if harmless, bangs from their rifles. They had firearms practice in the old brickyard on Sunday mornings. Charlie's patrol was the railway line, which he did between three and four in the morning, with his partner, Mr Miller. He did this for four years, and after patrol would have to come home to milk the cows and spend the day working the farm. On moonlit nights, the rails would gleam and make a perfect target for the Luftwaffe who were on their way to try to bomb Hullavington aerodrome. Charlie's saddest memory was of the day two British planes collided overhead in bad visibility. One of them, a Spitfire, came down in a field and couldn't stop. It hit a mound and somersaulted, killing the pilot.

During the war, prisoners of war from Germany and Italy could be hired from the Agricultural Committee to help with haymaking and harvesting. They would collect all the used binder twine, plait it and sew it together to make slippers to sell to the country folk. The Baker family at Angrove Farm used to come to us at Christmas for a party and they brought their Italian POW with them. He really enjoyed himself. One morning when Charlie went to fetch the cows, he was crossing the railway bridge just as a German plane flew in low overhead, firing at the train which was passing underneath. Charlie flung himself down in the ditch for

After war ended, Hullavington had an open day at the aerodrome. Charlie's sister, Matty, had married an airman called Leslie and this is their son, Kendal, with George. The children were allowed to take turns sitting in the planes and the boys were thrilled when it was their go.

safety and, luckily, both he and the cows escaped injury.

Evacuees from Gravesend in Essex were billeted on us - but their parents soon fetched them home when the bombing started! After they had gone, we had to let our spare rooms to war workers drafted into the area. New friends were made and visited us for many years to follow. We also had a young teacher from the village school lodged with us, and she still keeps in touch with me to this day.

When the homeguard was disbanded, the men had a huge party. They were all brought home in an old van and when the doors were opened, the effects of too much beer meant they all fell out of the back and into the mud in the road. They were so happy war was over they didn't care.

Hilda's husband, George Murray, was a schoolmaster in Malmesbury and got called up into the Army. This is him in his uniform before he got sent abroad. Hilda came to stay with me when he went away because she was pregnant but, sadly, had a miscarriage. Fortunately, George survived the war and came back to become headmaster of Alderbury School, just outside Salisbury.

Above: This is George and Anna with their great friends Elizabeth and Donald Baker from Angrove Farm, standing in our yard. Anna and Elizabeth met at school and Elizabeth would bring sandwiches for her lunch and eat them at our house because it was too far for her to walk home. As the boys got older they would all play together at our farm, or down at Angrove. They loved it down there because the farm had big old attics they could hide in.

Below: Here's George on an old trike that I got by trading a dozen eggs. George has always loved making things, and it must have started here because he added another wheel to the trike to give it four. Beside him is Anna on her roller skates. They're both out in the lane, where it was safe to play in those days.
Right: This is the swing Charlie rigged in the trees for the children. George, wearing one of my knitted pullovers, is on the swing with Anna behind him.

George made this Easter card for me at school.

THATCHING THE RICKS

Once the ricks had been built, they had to be thatched, to protect the hay from the rain. This was done by taking bundles of straw from the straw rick and weaving it into a roof on the hay rick to keep the harsh winter weather out.

To do this, Charlie had to cut spekes - pieces of wood, tapered at one end, about the size of a pencil - to push into the rick as anchors to twist the twine around. He would hold the straw in place, push in a speke, twist the twine around it, then push in another speke about eight inches away. He then pulled the twine across the straw and around the second speke, and so on, working his way around the rick.

The mangold and potato heaps also had to be thatched to keep the rain out. Here's Charlie thatching the hay rick after the spekes have been cut (left), and Anna and George with him up the ladder to keep him company.

He had a bill hook to whittle the spekes with. During the autumn, when he was out tending the hedges, he'd cut out nice pieces of nut wood (which was hard wearing) and put them to one side. Then, whenever he had a spare moment, he'd start to make the spekes.

This was a hot afternoon (right) because Charlie is sitting in the shade under the withy (willow) trees to cut the spekes. The children used to love to spend time with Charlie and were happy to be here, whiling away a pleasant afternoon with him. Dessie, our dog, was more interested in keeping the chickens at bay!

Left: Our children were given a couple of guinea pigs, which lived outdoors in the yard. They would wander freely around Rodbourne but always came home for their meal of bran. The two quickly multiplied to twenty-seven, and they became a familiar sight around the village.

Here's David Cole and his son on the tractor, Charlie on the reaping machine behind, and George standing by the tractor holding a rabbit that had got caught in the machinery. I took this in the early 1950s.

REAPING THE CORN

We still worked a crop rotation system at this time, which meant that cereal crops and root crops were not grown over and over again on the same patch of land. Our corn crop was a mixture of wheat, barley and oat fields.

After harvesting, all the corn usually went to make cattle feed for the winter, which saved us the expense of buying any. However, an exceptionally good crop would be sold back to the seed merchant to be used as the next year's seed and fetched a good price. Even so, some would be kept back to feed the cattle.

It was hard to produce a really good crop because there were so many variables. Rooks and pigeons were very fond of the new shoots - and could eat a surprising amount! Bad weather could ruin a harvest, and so on. If a crop was poor, it would mean parting with some hard earned cash from the sale of meat, eggs and milk, to replace the lost corn that would have gone to make the cattle feed.

Charlie was very proud of this oat crop (right) because we'd had a good summer, and the corn was good enough to be sold for seed. George and I made a special trip to the field so I could take this picture for posterity. Here, our wonderful crop is in stooks for drying.

Above: Harvest supper at Corston village hall; Charlie is sitting in the bottom right-hand corner, with David Cole and his wife beside him. On the top table you can see old Sir John Pollen sat next to Miss Luce, the church warden, (right) with the Reverend Anthony and his wife.

Below: David Cole and his tractor reaping the corn.

HARVEST TIME

Everyone lent a hand at harvesting time so that all would be gathered and stored before the bad weather set in. Mrs Macquillan (right)was the headmistress of Rodbourne School during the early 1950s and she and her husband, who's driving the tractor, were helping us bring the corn home. Anna and George came along for the ride. When all the preparations had been made to see us through the winter, we rewarded ourselves with a harvest supper. After the harvest festival Sunday service in the church,we held the supper in Corston village hall. We decorated the hall with flowers and sheaves of corn and laid out long trestle tables for the meal. Villagers would supply the tablecloths, cutlery and china, and we all tied different coloured cottons to our cutlery so we could identify it afterwards. The village women formed a committee to organise the food. Each woman would take charge of a particular dish and we'd have cooked hams, salads, mashed potatoes, home-made chutneys and pickles, followed by lovely dishes of trifle. After the vicar had said Grace, it was time to tuck in.

The children would have a tea party in the afternoon, then be sent to bed before the evening's festivities and speech-making began.

This was Charlie's 'farmer's mug' printed with the farmers' anthem on the back. He used it at home when he fancied a bottle of beer of an evening.

Here's George sitting on the vicarage lawn, blowing bubbles he'd won at the church fête.

THE CHURCH FETE

This was an annual summer treat and was held on the vicarage lawn at Corston. My friend Mary Salter and I would have a stall, there would be teas on the lawn and bowling for a young pig on display in a pen, given by one of the local farmers. There was also a fancy dress parade for the children. I always entered Anna and George for the competition and I think I enjoyed getting them ready as much as they enjoyed dressing up.

One year, Anna entered as Miss Wales, clutching a bunch of paper daffodils borrowed from the school. George was Aladdin. Luckily, I had the candlestick, and he wore my dressing gown as his robe. I plaited black wool for his pigtail and coloured his face with cold cream mixed with cocoa. They won first prize. Another year, Anna was a gypsy girl. She carried a doll as her baby and borrowed my shawl and basket of pegs. At this time, the gypsies still dressed very much like this. Again, she won first prize.

In the evening, when it was all over, a group of us used to walk back to Rodbourne and stop half-way at Tom Broom's pub, the Plough Inn. The men to enjoy their half pint of beer, the ladies a shandy, and the children lemonade and crisps. To us village folk, that was a lovely day.

Anna and George dressed for the competition as Miss Wales and Aladdin (right) and the gypsy girl (far right).

Old **Sir John Pollen died** in 1959 without any heirs, so his nephew, Captain Michael Pollen, took over the estate. We were all so used to saying 'Sir John', we referred to Michael as 'Sir John' too! When we first moved to Rodbourne, our next-door neighbour was Mr Cainey, gardener and chauffeur to the Miss Pollens (Sir John's aunts). When Mr Cainey died, the estate did his old house up. They needed land to go with the house because they wanted to sell it as a hunting lodge, so they took our home fields. When a farmer moved out, he was supposed to pay what was called 'dilapidation' money to the estate, but old Sir John said he'd waive that in our case if we let him have the ground, so we did. We gave up farming after that because we didn't have enough land to carry on.

This coincided with the new Tuberculosis Testing requirements introduced by the government - stating that new milking parlours must be built on all farms to meet the stricter guidelines for screening milk. The result of this law was that, throughout the country, small farms were amalgamated to create larger ones which made it more economical to implement the new building programme. Rodbourne was no exception, and our outer fields were divided amongst other farms nearby. Originally, there were six small farms in Rodbourne, now there are only three large ones.

Although we gave up farming in 1952, we stayed on in Pound Farm as a tenant cottage, and Charlie started contract work for some of the local farmers - John Baker at Angrove and David Cole, among others - for a weekly wage. He chiefly helped with harvesting, ploughing, haymaking and baling. I went out to work in the drawing library at E.K.C.O. (E.K. Cole) in Malmesbury. It was hard being shut indoors after my years out in the fields but I made lots of friends there, with whom I'm still in touch today.

When Anna left school, she came to work in the Personnel department at E.K.C.O. and we would occasionally meet for lunch. It was here that she met Jim, a Londoner working in Malmesbury, and they were married in Rodbourne Church in September, 1958. Earlier that year, Charlie had also come to work for the company, in the goods department. He would tease Jim for being a 'foreigner' - and continued to do so for years. To us village folk, no-one was considered local until they'd lived in the area for at least forty years!

My first grandchild, Sara Jane, was born in 1959, and grandson, Martin, came along in 1962. After Martin was born my son, George, finished his training at Redland Teacher Training Centre and went to Bermuda to teach (where he met his wife, Cathy). When he returned, he went off to teach in Sussex, then emigrated to Australia in 1973, where he still lives with Cathy and sons, Colin and Marcos, and teaches at Bundaberg North High School.

Charlie hated being cooped up inside after years of farm work and eventually left E.K.C.O. to work at Malmesbury School. This job suited him down to the ground. The school kept cattle and other animals and he used to look after them, and tend the gardens. He was there until he retired in 1976.

Throughout this time, although we were working in town, we continued our country existence at Pound Farm. In the evenings, I would tend my lovely garden - like Confucius, I believed that if a man has two loaves of bread he should sell one and buy flowers to nourish his soul. Evenings were also devoted to our walks. When the children were younger, we would all sit very quietly under a hedge where there was a fox earth adjoining a badger sett and were thrilled to have both kinds of cubs come up to us if we kept perfectly still. Another day, we'd see hares sitting up on their hind legs having a boxing match. Occasionally a deer would stray from a neighbouring estate and cross our path.

I was always drawn in to accompany my son, and later my grandson, to tramp the fields in search of exhibits for the school nature table. Sometimes, we would take a sack and collect dry wood for the fires. There were lots of slow worms, which looked like small snakes, around the garden and grandson, Martin, would come in with them coiled up his arms. In spring, in the marshier areas, we'd spot cuckoo flowers, ragged robins and wild orchids and, by the stream, sunny clumps of marsh marigold. Birds would be building their nests everywhere and the dawn chorus, around 4am, was wonderful.

On November 5, everybody would bring their fireworks to the village bonfire on the grass verge near Church Farm. The children had a great time eating the refreshments around the bonfire. In the early 1950s, there was no TV, so Dorothy Payne would organise a Beetle Drive especially for the children - for which we paid a small charge that usually went to the church. There was a table and chairs for four in all the rooms at Manor Farm. Play would start in the scullery and the two who won the first game would move on up the back stairs to the first bedroom, and so it progressed all through the upstairs rooms and then downstairs.

Christmas brought the school concert and parties. All the villagers really enjoyed the concerts, so they were always well attended. Mothers had to get busy and help make the costumes. One year, Anna was the Virgin Mary and George a shepherd. Another year, the vicar dressed as Father Christmas and walked past the school windows with a sack on his back, leading a donkey which had reindeer horns attached to its head. Anna and George used to save their money and I would take them to Chippenham or Swindon to do their Christmas shopping. They took such pleasure in wrapping those presents and attaching their own home-made Christmas cards.

Also on winter nights we'd have village friends in to play cards, while the children played Snap or Ludo, and finish the evening with refreshments. When I was a child, my stern father never allowed us to have friends in the house or to give birthday parties, so I took good care that my own children and grandchildren knew the joy of bringing friends to supper or to stay for the weekend.

In 1966, Charlie and I took our first trip abroad. I had gone along to the travel agency with George, who was planning to go to Iceland. While we were there, the travel agent encouraged me to go to Austria and, before I knew it, I'd booked twelve days there on a coach trip. Charlie and I were very excited about our holiday and he suggested I buy a new camera to take colour slides while we were there. I gave George a cheque and he came home with an Ilford Sportsman. I wished I'd had a few days to practise with it before we went away because I found the light meter and focusing very complicated and ruined the first few rolls of

film! Having said that, we had a wonderful holiday and eventually managed to master the camera and got some lovely pictures. I took colour photographs from then on. The following year, we went on a similar trip to Norway - and loved that too.

Sundays were still our favourite time for days out in the car and we'd travel the countryside, visiting neighbouring villages and beauty spots where we'd stop for our picnic tea. As our grandchildren grew older, we'd all go out together as a family - they were such lovely times.

I left work in the early 1960s and devoted my time to tending the garden, and continued to make jams, chutneys and so on, the way I used to when we were still farming. I also did a lot of knitting for my grandchildren, who often used to come and stay with us.

My Ilford Sportsman camera, bought by George in 1966.

We left Pound Farm in 1976 and moved to Malmesbury because my daughter, Anna, thought it was high time we had a few mod cons. There were no shops in Rodbourne, and the farm still had a bucket lavatory outside, no bathroom, no central heating - just open fires - and the range in the kitchen to cook on. The first thing I bought for our new home was a bath mat!

We had accumulated a lot of things over forty years at the farm, so Charlie had a bonfire going for a week before we left. My granddaughter, Sara, still winces when she hears about the things we burned, but we moved to a much smaller place and had no room for it all. My friend Mary Salter had already moved to Malmesbury and encouraged us to join her. The Reynolds' and other friends had also left Rodbourne by this time.

After we moved to Malmesbury, we still spent as much time as possible outdoors. We planted vegetables, herbs and flowers in the garden, spent Sundays out in the car and enjoyed walking around the town.

Needless to say, among the things that escaped the bonfire and came with us, were my trusty camera and photographs!

Above: **When we moved into Pound Farm, the kitchen window was obscured by the box hedge which was about 6ft high. Charlie cut it down and I took to doing the flower garden. The two tubs by the gate were made from an old barrel that Charlie cut in half. I planted all the daffodils which still come up every spring.**

Above: **The hedge in front of the porch was covered in honeysuckle which I planted when I first moved in.**

Left: **My Epiphyllum cactus on the ledge of the dining room window.**

Poppies and Whitsuntide Stock

This was the border on one of my lawns. It brings back memories of sunny Sunday afternoons, a picnic tea on the grass, a piece of net or lace curtain stretched between two sticks and a game of 'tennis' with the grandchildren. At a farm sale I bought a bundle of badminton racquets which vastly improved our game. How we all enjoyed it. Charlie had also put a swing in an apple tree for our children and grandchildren. Often, the tea party would be near the pond so the young ones could enjoy the antics of the moorhens and their brood of chicks.

I always loved the large red poppies. Their petals looked as though they were made from crumpled tissue paper with black velvet for the centres. I longed for some in my garden. When I mentioned this to my friend Betty, she brought me a root and told me that from then on I'd never be without them. How right she was. They seemed to be indestructible. I picked them when the green bud was just bursting and showing the crumpled red. I burnt the ends of the stems and they opened out in the vase, looking very majestic.

Mixed in with the poppies, the highly scented white and mauve Whitsuntide stock made a wonderful show for this picture.

Beside the back door (below) is the extra window we had put in to make the sitting room lighter. Where the flower border is here, there used to be a pile of ashes and rubbish about ten feet long where the people who lived here before used to bury the contents of their lavatory bucket! I didn't want that outside my back door so we levelled it off, turned the earth over, and grew marvellous flowers. On the right is a wicket gate which led under an ash archway to another garden. A bank ran along the edge of the flower border and I planted a hedge on the top of it to make a nice, private area. At the end of the bank were four big elm trees, where George used to have a tree house when he was a boy.

Right: This was the kitchen door, which had a beautiful Albertine rose growing over it. The people who lived here before us never used it, but we opened it up. Flycatchers used to nest in the rose every year and, without fail, a cuckoo would lay an egg in that nest. Very soon the cuckoo egg would hatch and the poor baby flycatchers would be turfed out. The young cuckoo gorged all the food so painstakingly found by the adoptive parents. When it was ready to leave the nest it would sit on our row of kidney bean sticks and keep up an eternal squawk for food, keeping the foster parents very busy. Under the window is an old fashioned sweet pea which came up yearly.

This is Frank Reynolds driving his
tractor past the school on a frosty
winter's morning. He was taking his
empty milk churns up to his farm
ready for the night's milking.
Sadly, at haymaking time, Frank was
killed in a tragic accident. It is
thought that when he got down off
the tractor, the brake slipped and
the vehicle and its loaded wagon of
hay ran over him.

Right: When we got married in 1937, it was the jubilee of King George V and Queen Mary. Back in Malmesbury, my old cat had given birth. We took one tabby and one black and white and christened them George and Mary. This Mary was one of their descendants. She was lovely and had lots of kittens of her own. She enjoyed sitting in the sun and looking out for the rare passer-by. I always knew if it was a dog because she'd arch her back and spit furiously. Here, she's keeping watch at the dining room window. In it, you can see a reflection of the elm trees that stood up on Frank Reynolds' bank.

Above: This is Tom on the lawn at Pound Farm. He's got rusty patches that are separate to the tabby pattern on his coat. That's because one cold morning he sat too close to the one-bar electric fire in the kitchen and got scorched. We always had lovely cats. Tom's probably about six here. He was a real farm cat. We had several like him, one after the other. When George was a boy, his tabby went missing and he went to find him. The cat had been run over by a train while out rabbiting along the railway line. George brought home the tail and hind-quarters to give him a 'proper' burial!

Miss Atherton Brown was our next-door neighbour. She was born on a big estate like Badminton Park and her father owned lots of racehorses. After her parents died, she came to live in Rodbourne. She heard about the house from Captain Mark Phillips' parents who had looked at it for themselves but found it too small.

Beside Miss Brown is Miss Smith (above) who was her nanny. She'd been with her ever since Miss Brown was six years old, and she died aged ninety five. If Miss Brown ever went away, I used to go and babysit Miss Smith.

Miss Brown was a lovely person and loved her dogs. That's Mustard jumping outside the front of Miss Brown's house. I was trying to get a picture of him but I didn't realise he was going to jump so high! She is in the background and had just thrown that little yellow ball for him. Miss Brown used to go to the hunt balls, and would give dinner parties beforehand and I used to go over to help her out with the food. She was also our local Church Warden for many years.

This old wheelbarrow was left by some workmen in return for all the welcome cups of tea and home-made cake I had given them. Tom thought it made a very good resting place. We used it for mucking out the cow sheds, stables and fowl houses. If the tyre was soft it was mighty heavy going when full. It also came in useful at apple picking time for taking the fruit to the back door. Once upstairs, the apples were carefully stored in a spare room for use in winter. A naughty mouse would often find them and nibble away until only the skins were left. Tom should have been keeping guard instead of lounging in the barrow. I've had that wheelbarrow for fifty six years - it still sits in my garden today.

Above: This is the entrance to Rodbourne churchyard. Those crocuses come out every February. Someone had at one time planted a dozen of the bulbs on the grave on the left. They spread like wildfire and ran all along the path. They've even gone onto the verge outside now. On the right are quite a few Punter graves. They were the oldest family in Rodbourne.

This was a beautiful Autumn day and the oak tree was absolutely gold with the sun on it (above). I was standing on the right, just by Miss Brown's place, to take the picture. In the background you can see the school. The children used to play out on the grass and do their country dancing in the playground in front. When our children were small, we used to go to all the school concerts and plays.

The school porch (right) carries the words: *'Come unto me ye children and I will teach ye the words of the Lord'* carved beneath a frame of acorns and oak leaves. This was the work of the estate carpenter, George Punter, in around 1850. He was the great grandfather of my husband Charlie. During the mid-1800s, the village was in the hands of John Hungerford Pollen, a respected member of the Pre-Raphaelite group and one of the most noted seceders from the Church of England to that of Rome. We imagine that he would have influenced the work of George Punter. Appropriately, a sculptor and family live there now.

MICHAELMAS DAISIES

I had a lovely garden at Rodbourne and really enjoyed tending it. With my camera ever to hand I captured this beautiful Red Admiral butterfly, and the bees in almost every centre of the Michaelmas daisies, enjoying the sunshine and pollen.

In the backround on the right is Anna's first Christmas tree. We planted it in 1939 and now it stands as tall as the house. The double pink cherry tree with the school behind it was a great favourite. George bought it with his first set of wages and I planted it in 1967. It stood at the back gate.

The garden was a peaceful place, with lawns and flower borders and several large trees. You could pass from the first part through a little wicket gate and ash archway - made by bending the young tree over to meet the yellow winter jasmine and highly scented old pink rose, Zephrine Drouhin - into another part of the garden. There, you found more lawn and flower borders, the old Codlin apple tree, several Victoria plum trees and the vegetable garden.

Going on round the front of the house, with its lovely old porch covered in old-fashioned roses, you went past the dairy and a hollow tree stump filled with flowers. An elder tree was planted near the dairy to ward off witches who could turn the milk sour - or so the old folk used to say. Continuing past the old six foot high box bush hedge - where the guinea fowl nested and acted as guards to let us know when anyone was approaching - through another wicket gate, and you were back to where you started!

Michaelmas daisies always remind me of harvest festival. Mothers and children used to arrive at church on Saturday mornings with armfuls of flowers for decoration. The men folk would stagger behind with wheelbarrows filled with fruit and vegetables and sheaves of corn. The church used to look beautiful and was always packed for harvest festival. How often I have sat there and taken comfort from the words over the altar:

'Fear not, for I am with
you even unto the end'.

We also used Michaelmas daisies at Anna and Jim's September wedding reception in the village school.

MITZI AND THE KNITTING

I **had been sitting** in that deckchair in the back garden, knitting a pullover for Charlie and listening to the radio which was a present from a friend who moved to Canada. The cat is Mitzi, and she had settled down so beautifully in my knitting I couldn't resist taking the picture. When I used to take the Kodak Magazine it advised readers not to go anywhere without a camera - because you never knew when you might see something you'd want to photograph. Still heeding their advice, I was ready and able to take this picture.

The withy (willow) trees in the background cast a lovely shade in the summer and grew from sticks stuck in the ground by Charlie before the war. He cut them on one of his regular journeys bringing the cows back from the fields. A pretty white rambler rose grew up the trunk amongst the branches of one.

I love cows. I took a picture of this one because it looked like one of our herd. You don't see many mixed Short-horns any more, and that's what we used to have. I managed to get nice and close to her to take this and I think her expression is lovely.

Right: After Frank Reynolds' tragic accident with his tractor, Charlie used to help his widow, Doris, and son, Edward, with work at Church Farm. This is Charlie with some of their cows at the back of their barn.

Above: I went out and took this early one morning while Charlie was having his breakfast because the light was so lovely. It wasn't a heavy snowfall but it looked so beautiful and I knew if I waited it would be gone - it was already melting on the road. I stood near the church to capture this view.

Edward Reynolds (below) was a good neighbour. He'd come to cut some wood for us. There is Charlie on the right and Stuart Barton - Lucy's husband - on the left, holding the wood.

After Edward's father Frank was killed, he and his wife Margaret, baby Mark and mother Doris, found a small tenant farm in Carmarthen, Wales. They had to load all of their cattle, farm machinery and household contents and make the long journey to their new home, stopping halfway to rest the cattle and arriving late in the evening. When they arrived they had to unload their cattle and immediately start milking.

Edward, Margaret and Mark made a success of their new farm and have since bought it. They still return and visit their friends in the area.

Right: This is the old Buttercross. Behind it are two houses. The one on the right was the village post office and on the left was Frank Reynolds' place, Church Farm.

My friend Mary Salter lived on the right, and the post office was in her sitting room. It was only open for a few hours each day. There used to be a little red letter box on a post outside on the grass verge. If you took a letter to Mary, you had to knock on the front door and you'd be asked into the sitting room to do your business. When the post office closed, the house remained as Mary's home. If you lived along the top road in Rodbourne you got an afternoon post - but if you lived off that road, as we did, you had to wait until the next morning.

Next door lived the Reynolds family. Doris was from Manchester and came to work as a land girl during the war. There were three land girls who worked on Greenhill's farm at Rodbourne Bottom - and they all married local boys.

The age of this Buttercross isn't known. There's no writing on it. It was named after villagers from past centuries who would stop here, on their way to market with butter and eggs, to pray. The steps are worn from the feet of several generations - including those of the Rodbourne schoolchildren who used to love to clamber over here and play.

It was flanked by four beautiful big elm trees, which fell victim to Dutch Elm disease. You can see the evidence of that here.

Herds of cows used to be driven through Rodbourne to grazing - even in the 1960s - and their tracks cut clearly through the foreground. Rodbourne was known as the Place of Mud in those days, but we were so used to it we didn't take any notice.

The elms are long gone - though Sir John has since planted four new trees to replace them.

STUART AND LUCY AT RODBOURNE BOTTOM

The front path leading to Godwin's Farm, where the flower borders bear testimony to Lucy's green fingers.

Stuart and Lucy Barton lived down at Rodbourne Bottom, near Greenhill's farm. Lucy was a great gardener. She was very artistic and did beautiful painting and embroidery, and taught at Rodbourne school. She did all the gardening at Godwin's Farm. These pictures were taken in the early 1960s before she fell victim to Parkinson's Disease. Her son Ben (my nephew) lives here still - and is the last remaining member of the old Rodbourne community.

Stuart's father was very fond of cricket and formed a Rodbourne team, for which Charlie used to play. Charlie said Stuart's father would leave a field of hay to spoil rather than miss out on his cricket! Stuart's mother was a tall, slim woman and used to drive a pony and trap around the village and into Malmesbury. One day she collided with old Sir John in a lane and he took the wheel off her trap with his car.

The back garden of Godwin's Farm was beautiful. The house, like ours, was big but basic. There were no bathrooms even then - just a bucket lavatory and one cold tap. People made their gardens attractive to compensate. Lucy spent lots of time on hers. The little juniper tree is one I brought back for her from Norway. The path leads on into the farmyard where Lucy kept a lot of geese - they made good watchdogs. You can just see one in the background. Lucy died in the 1980s - but had kept gardening right up until the time her disease finally got the better of her.

Overleaf: When the river flooded - as it still used to in the 1960s - Stuart would get trapped on his side of the lane. I went down there to see what the floods were like. The river had come up so quickly it had washed all the dried hay away. At this stage, Stuart couldn't get through, and we had to shout at each other across the water.

This is the back of Stuart and Lucy's house, awash with colour thanks to Lucy's gardening skills.

DUTCH ELM DISEASE STRIKES

Workmen were finally called in to fell the elms - all of which were riddled with the fatal Dutch Elm disease.

On the left, you can see the results of the Dutch Elm disease that swept the village. The large tree on the right was just below our house at the edge of our home field. When the children were babies I put them out there to sleep in their prams. We didn't want to lose the elm trees because it would change the landscape so dramatically, but every elm in the village had to be felled.

Our house is in the background of the right-hand picture. Charlie, and Jack Payne with his dog, are watching the elms being felled. Our bucket lavatory was situated under those trees and, before Dutch Elm disease had really taken hold, Charlie went in there and - to his horror - saw the ground moving beneath his feet! He reported it to Sir John who called in the experts. They detected the rot and felled the trees. They did this by cutting a 'V' shape into the trunk until the tree keeled over. I used to go round afterwards and collect the chippings for our fire.

The bucket lavatory was at the end of a long muddy path. The road outside was higher, so when it rained the water and mud swept down the bank into our loo. When we paid the rent at Sir John's kitchen door, I told the estate agent that our bucket was wearing out - hoping that we might get a bathroom. The next time I saw him, he said: "I've got good news for you". I crossed my fingers.

He went on: "I've got the last lavatory bucket on sale in Malmesbury". So much for a bathroom! I had to cart that thing back through the village to our place and we had it until the day we moved out in 1976.

I've always been a WI member. It was a wonderful way of bringing country women together. Mary Salter once told me she didn't know how to make plum jam until she joined. This was the Corston and Rodbourne WI. Mrs Hastings was president, but even when she wasn't she still had us over to her place for tea for a summer meeting. We'd take our own cups to save her washing up and she'd give us buttered buns and a lovely assortment of cakes and tea. All the WI meetings would end with the social half hour. For hers, she would match buttons to the colours of the flowers and hide them. The person who found the most buttons won. Here, members are searching diligently for the coveted prize of a headscarf.

I used to belong to the Mothers Union which was affiliated to the Church. It was formed to promote the sanctity of marriage. Chad Vara's wife was head of the Mothers Union when I was there, and he was the man who started the Samaritans.

I had our summer meeting in our garden. We started with a hymn and a prayer, taken by Reverend Taylor on the lawn. Then he introduced our speaker, Mrs Richards, and we finished with a hymn and a prayer. Everyone enjoyed walking around our garden after I had brought out the tea.

The Reverend Taylor was lovely. He was editor of the Wiltshire News before he became a vicar. He's with Mrs Harold Miles, the two Miss Slades from Corston, Peggy Taylor, Dorothy Freeth, our president Mrs Holbrow, Mrs Richards in green hat and coat who gave the talk, Mrs Rudman, Tess Frayling, and some members from the neighbouring village of Lea. Members took it in turns to host these meetings.

I remember this walk well. Charlie had not been well and decided the cure was a country walk. Having an open fire, we never left dry wood hanging around - hence the enormous stick he is carrying. It was Autumn 1970. Our journey had taken us through our old fields, which adjoined the railway line. Those men working in the fields who didn't own a watch set their time by the trains. There was always one at dinner time and another when it was time to bring the cows home for milking. On this walk, we had our first glimpse of Concorde.

This was taken from George's bedroom window. He was in his twenties
by this time and had left college and gone to Bermuda to teach. I sent
this picture to him to remind him of home. I used to come up here with
Charlie's binoculars and on a fine day I could see the white horse on
Cherhill. It was a beautiful view.

I took this from our bedroom window and sent it to George to show him
the garden. I had an old chair by this window and used to sit there to do
my sewing and writing. This was late summer, it had been a dry time
because the fields are brown. Beyond you can see the Reynolds' farm, and
the railway line in the distance.

Here's my granddaughter, Sara, on the road to Heath Cleeves. She was pointing to all the birds going to roost in the wood. There has always been a great bonding between us because Sara came to stay with me when her brother Martin was born. We used to go on long walks every Sunday and this was early evening on one of those walks. She loved being here so much she didn't want to go home.

THE HUNTING SEASON

The beagle season was in winter. They met once a year at Rodbourne. They ran after the hares and the men would follow on foot. There were the Eton College beagles, the Cirencester College beagles and the Dauntsey Vale beagles - who, unlike the others, were kept by farmers. The men wore knee breeches, knee socks and stout shoes. The villagers would follow behind.

The Beaufort hunt used to meet in the village about twice during the season and lots of the villagers would follow the horses and hounds on foot. This was in the days before the anti-hunting campaigners became so vocal.

Our outlook was tempered by life in the country where the fox was considered a pest. Most villagers kept poultry and relied on the sale of eggs and fattened birds at Christmas to help supplement their meagre incomes.

We were never able to take firm orders for turkeys as the fox would often get an early Christmas feast. Also, turkeys were very hard to rear and many died of fright after the fox had had his fun, or they contracted diseases which killed them.

Our old black labrador, Toby, seemed to know when the hunt was coming. He would sit on the hayrick and howl all night. In the morning he would stride up to the hounds and the old Duke of Beaufort, who knew him well, would say: "Ah, here comes Toby". Charlie still used to follow the hounds on his old bike when he was well into his eighties, with a little flask of whisky to keep out the cold.

Right: The beagles gathered ready to hunt hares on a cold winter's day.

Overleaf: The men in red coats were visitors to the Beaufort hunt from the Vale of White Horse hunt. They would pay for a day's fox hunting with another pack to enable them to qualify to ride at the local point-to-point races later in the season.

This was late afternoon in Avebury - a village set in a huge circle of stones that are in a line with Stonehenge. There's a lovely feeling when you walk amongst those stones. Charlie and I often went there - it was one of our favourite haunts. The downs in the background are the same ones you can see from George's window in Rodbourne.

This is Arlington Row in Bibury, taken on one of our trips out on a Sunday afternoon. That's why so many of my pictures have that lovely, late afternoon light. I always take peaceful scenes and I love the way the afternoon glow seems to enhance the atmosphere of serenity.

FAVOURITE DAYS OUT

Whenever the weather was nice, Charlie and I used to like to get in the car and head for some of the beauty spots nearby. This was usually on a Sunday. Charlie didn't like to miss his Sunday roast, so we'd eat at midday and go off in the afternoons, taking a big picnic tea with us.

I always had my camera, of course, and would often persuade Charlie to stop if I saw something I wanted to photograph en route. I had to be quick though, because he didn't like turning the car round if we'd driven past! We visited many of the pretty old-fashioned villages in our area, where I took some of my favourite pictures.

When my niece, Glenna, was going to Australia, she bought a film and asked me to take some pictures of Malmesbury. She wanted to take them to show her elderly aunts, who were already living out there. Whichever way you enter Malmesbury you come down a hill, across a bridge over a river and up a hill. It's called the town on the hill. I walked everywhere I could think of and took lots of lovely views.

This (right) is along Burnivale. You can see the steeple, and the abbey over to the left. That's Anna sitting on the steps. Again it's in the late aftenoon light I'm so fond of.

This is my granddaughter, Sara, at a traction engine steam rally. She looked so happy and I liked to photograph her doing things she enjoyed. She was about nine at the time and thought she was the bees knees. I used to go to church on Sunday mornings, then Charlie and I would go out with the family in the afternoons.

Above: This is Fiona Sillars, the doctor's daughter, taken in 1977.
That year she was Carnival Queen. In the background, the men are
getting ready for the lawnmower race. Sister Julian entered; she
had the little Abbey House hand-mower and was running with it,
habit flying - the other competitors drove theirs!
I still enter the Carnival with the Malmesbury WI float.

Above: This is one of my very favourite pictures. It really is peaceful. It's taken in Brokenborough - a lovely little village a couple of miles from Malmesbury. The dear little bridge was the centre of attraction. I love taking bridges. You can stand on this one and watch the trout swimming lazily underneath. I wanted to capture the light on the water, and the beautiful colours. It was just lovely.

Left: Every year we go to the Malmesbury Carnival at the end of August. Here's Sara and brother Martin entering as 'The Surrey With The Fringe On Top', back in the 1960s. They won second prize. George made the white horse out of wire netting and sheets. The cart used to be George's pram. He turned it into a racing car when he was a boy, then it did service again as the 'surrey'. While the children were waiting to be judged a tall man dressed as a Dalek stood nearby. Martin was supposed to be 'guarding' Sara, he had his gun and everything, but he was scared stiff of the Dalek - he thought it was real!